Care and Identification of 19th-Century Photographic Prints

By James M. Reilly

Care and Identification of

19th-Century Photographic Prints

By JAMES M. REILLY

With Research Assistance
and Selection of Photographic Illustrations
by Constance McCabe

CARE AND IDENTIFICATION OF
19TH-CENTURY PHOTOGRAPHIC PRINTS

Editor:
Joan C. Matochik

Book Design:
D. Malczewski

Cover Photograph:
Salted Paper Print
Probably of English Origin,
Late 1850s
Photographer Unknown
Courtesy of the International Museum
of Photography at the George Eastman House (IMP/GEH)

Photomacrographs:
Caterina Salvi at the Biomedical Photographic
Communications Laboratory, Rochester Institute
of Technology

KODAK Publication No. G-2S
CAT Softcover 160 7787
Library of Congress Catalog Card No. 85-081727
ISBN 0-87985-365-4
Printed in the United States of America

About the Author

James M. Reilly is a member of the faculty of Rochester Institute of Technology, Rochester, New York. He is director of the newly-created Image Permanence Institute, a testing and research laboratory jointly sponsored by The Society of Photographic Scientists and Engineers and RIT. Professor Reilly has been a consultant on photographic preservation to numerous museums and institutions and is active on Subcommittees of the American National Standards Institute dealing with photographic image stability. He is also a member of the Photographic Materials Group of the American Institute for Conservation. Professor Reilly has written a number of technical papers on photographic preservation and is the author of *The Albumen and Salted Paper Book: The History and Practice of Photographic Printing 1840–1895,* published in 1980 by Light Impressions Corp.

ACKNOWLEDGEMENTS

Few technical books are really the work of one person, but this book has benefited more than usual from the help and suggestions of others. Constance McCabe helped to conceive it, organize it, critique it, and did much of the work of selecting and creating its illustrations. Together we made many refinements and improvements in the *IDENTIFICATION GUIDE*, enough so that the finished product would have been far inferior without her help.

A special debt of gratitude is owed to John Sippel, who saw a friendly offer of help turn into a major volunteer effort. He took a handwritten manuscript, entered it into a word processor, then helped to clarify and organize it. I shall always be grateful for this expert help, so unselfishly given.

The sponsors of this book are the federal grant agencies that made it possible to do the research which underlies it. They are: The National Museum Act (administered by the Smithsonian Institution), the National Historical Publications and Records Commission (administered by the National Archives), and the National Endowment for the Humanities. Anyone who finds this book useful will join me in thanking them for their concern for our photographic heritage.

I thank the Eastman Kodak Company for its role in publishing this book. It, too, demonstrates a concern for the cultural patrimony that photography represents. Particular thanks must go to Allie C. Peed Jr., Kenneth T. Lassiter, Paul F. Mulroney Jr., George Eaton, Joan Matochik, and Dan Malczewski for their contributions. At the Kodak Research Laboratories, I thank Donald Black and Ted Van Dam both for their excellent work in electron microscopy and their interest in this project.

Others who have helped in the creation of the manuscript include my wife, Linda Reilly, Nora Kennedy, Grant Romer, Douglas Severson, Debora Bork, Debbie Hess Norris, James Lewis, Gerald Munoff, and numerous professionals who took the time to criticize an outline and suggest inclusions.

The fine photomacrographs which appear in this book are the work of Caterina Salvi, who also gave generously of her skills and time. David Kolody made it possible to illustrate this book with instructive (yet visually interesting) examples of processes and deterioration. To the administration of the George Eastman House I owe thanks for permission to use images from their collection. Especially helpful were David Wooters, Barbara Galasso, and Linda McCausland. Similar thanks also extend to the Art Institute of Chicago and the Wallace Memorial Library at RIT.

Finally, I thank Rochester Institute of Technology for its support of research and programs in photographic preservation. I am especially grateful to Dr. Russell C. Kraus, former Director of RIT's School of Photographic Arts and Sciences, for his encouragement at every stage of this project.

James M. Reilly

Rochester, New York
February, 1986

TABLE OF CONTENTS

Chapter III:

Chapter IV:

INTRODUCTION

For many reasons we have come to value photographic images which survive from the 19th century. Most of these are prints, the normal end product of photography; the survival of a negative is fortunate but comparatively rare. This book is concerned with the identification and preservation of 19th-century photographic prints.

In order to preserve prints we need to understand them as physical objects and learn how to use them in ways that do not contribute to their destruction. Photographic preservation is a relatively new field of study, and there is much left to discover about the proper care and storage of 19th-century print materials. Nineteenth-century print processes are too complex and varied to allow for blanket pronouncements about the causes or remedies of deterioration. Each of the major processes needs to be subjected to scientific investigation, from which specific preservation recommendations can be derived.

The impetus for this book was provided by just such an intensive investigation of the albumen print, which was by far the most popular of the 19th-century print materials. From 1978 to 1982, the preservation problems of albumen prints were the sub-

ject of research at Rochester Institute of Technology in Rochester, New York. This research, under the direction of the author, was funded by grants from the National Endowment for the Humanities (Research Resources Program), the National Museum Act (administered by the Smithsonian Institution), and the National Historical Publications and Records Commission. Its goal was to lay the groundwork for improved preservation methods by determining the rate-controlling factors in albumen print deterioration.

An important aspect of the research was to be the incorporation of its findings into a handbook for the care of albumen prints in collections. The Eastman Kodak Company has cooperated in that effort to make possible this book, which not only incorporates the information gained from the albumen research, but also attempts to summarize the available preservation information for other important 19th-century print materials.

Given their popularity, it is appropriate that much of the specific information provided here concerns albumen prints—but other types of prints also need to undergo careful scientific investigation. For them, while we await further research, we can only provide assistance in process identification and a summary of their known preservation needs. Even for albumen prints, there are many unanswered questions.

This book is intended for anyone with a collection of 19th-century photographic prints. Whether a collection consists of one print or a hundred thousand, a family album or an entire state archive, the technical basis of preservation will be the same; only the scale of operations will differ.

Restoration is not touched upon in this book. There is actually very little that can be done to reverse deterioration in print materials, and all such attempts are the proper domain of a trained professional conservator. The owners and custodians of photographic collections have a more important role: to store and use their collections in ways that prevent or retard further deterioration. The information herein can help in that task.

Photographic collections differ greatly in size, significance, and purpose. Each collection must cope with a different set of environmental conditions and preservation problems. In addition, the resources devoted to preserving a given set of photographs are almost never entirely adequate to the task, making it inevitable that every owner or custodian of a collection will need to make some preservation compromises in the light of that collection's unique priorities, circumstances, and limitations.

This book consistently advocates the highest level of care, and does not attempt to provide specific guidelines for making preservation compromises. There are two reasons for this approach: first, because even a book several times the length of this one could not adequately deal with the limitless variables encountered in different collections; and second, because compromises in preservation policy should always be shaped by an awareness of the most satisfactory approach to a problem.

It should, however, be noted that the one area in which compromises are least acceptable is in establishing safe environmental conditions, particularly with respect to relative humidity. Beyond that, successful preservation depends mostly on the people who care for—and care about—a collection. Taking a little extra time to put a print away or caring enough to notice that a print is torn is the kind of indispensable human contribution that can ultimately make the difference in the survival of photographic images.

XII

Chapter I:

THE HISTORY OF PHOTOGRAPHIC PRINTING IN THE 19TH CENTURY

Any preservation effort should begin with an understanding of what one is trying to preserve. A knowledge of the historical development of photographic print processes during the 19th century is directly useful for dating photographs and for process identification. It forms a foundation and context for much of the specific preservation data mentioned later in this book.

THE EARLIEST PHOTOGRAPHIC PRINTS: PHOTOGENIC DRAWINGS

From its experimental beginnings in the 1830s and on through the 19th century, photographic printing relied mainly on the light sensitivity of silver compounds. It had long been known that silver compounds tend to darken when exposed to light, but not until 1839 did a satisfactory and practical print process appear. In announcing his *photogenic drawing* process,

essential contribution was to identify silver chloride as the silver compound most suitable for photographic printing, and to discover how to use it most effectively.

The photogenic drawing had three essential ingredients: a sheet of paper, sodium chloride (table salt), and silver nitrate. A sheet of fine quality writing paper was soaked in a dilute sodium chloride solution, then dried. By treating the sheet with a strong silver nitrate solution, silver chloride was formed and the paper became sensitive to light. The key factor in the process was the relative proportion of chloride and silver. Talbot was the first to understand that an excess of silver was required for maximum sensitivity. The sensitized paper darkened rapidly when exposed to direct sunlight or daylight. The image appeared spontaneously during exposure, without needing chemical development. Papers of this type are known as *printing-out papers*, as op-

Timeline of Major Photographic Print Processes

1840	1860	1880	1900	1920	1940	1960	1980

1840–55 Salted Paper Prints

1855–95 Albumen Prints

1895–1905 Gelatin and Collodion Printing-Out Prints

1905–60 Gelatin Developing-Out Prints

1960– Chromogenic Color Prints

William Henry Fox Talbot provided the essential technology for creating silver images on paper. Photogenic drawings, though very rare, are the ultimate ancestors and archetypes for all of the silver printing-out papers used during the 19th century. Talbot's

posed to *developing-out papers*, where chemical treatment is required to make the image visible.

The photogenic drawing process was first used to create images of leaves, engravings, lace, and other objects by placing them directly on

This timeline shows the major photographic print processes throughout the history of photography.

Silver Printing-Out Papers

Paper Darkens on
Exposure to Daylight
NO Chemical
Development

Toning Optional
Development
Not Required

Brown or Purple
Image Color

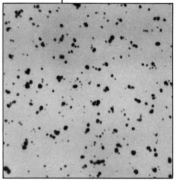

Enlarged 40,000X,
the image consists of
small round silver particles.

---

sensitized paper. When the exposure was complete, a method was needed for removing or inactivating the unexposed silver chloride. The method used to "fix" the print differentiates a photogenic drawing from its direct lineal descendant, the salted paper print. In the early years of experimentation with photogenic drawing, Talbot was unaware of sodium thiosulfate or "hypo," the substance which soon came into general use as a fixing agent. For photogenic drawings, Talbot used a concentrated sodium chloride solution which gave images a purplish-brown color, with pale "lilac" non-image areas. Because the silver chloride was merely inactivated by excess chloride and not actually removed, photogenic drawings are unstable and may still be somewhat sensitive to light.

SALTED PAPER PRINTS: 1840–1855

In the photogenic drawing process, Talbot had found a way to make positive prints, but he encountered only frustration in trying to use the method to produce negatives in the camera. The year 1841 saw all this change in

light of two very significant discoveries: a revolutionary method of making negatives by chemical development and the transformation of the photogenic drawing process into what we now call the *salted paper print*. With the invention of his *calotype*, or paper negative process, Talbot converted photography into a two-step operation involving *a negative* image with

Salted paper was the earliest photographic print process of major importance. This is a French example from the early 1850s.

IMP/GEH

2

Silver Developing-Out Papers

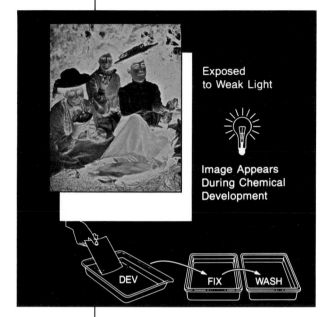

Exposed to Weak Light

Image Appears During Chemical Development

DEV FIX WASH

Neutral Black
Image Color

Enlarged 40,000X,
the image consists of
clumps of filamentary silver.

reversed tones, from which any number of *positive*, tonally correct copies could be made. The advantage of the negative/positive approach to photography was that it allowed the easy multiplication of photographic images.

At almost the same time, Talbot materially improved the technique of making positive prints by adopting a new method of fixing photogenic drawings. It was Sir John F. W. Herschel who first suggested the use of "hyposulphite of soda" as a fixing agent. Hypo actually removes silver chloride, providing a more stable and satisfactory print, and its use as a fixer became almost universal after 1841. With the substitution of hypo for the strong salt solutions used to fix photogenic drawings, the salted paper print was born, and Talbot now had a perfect medium for making positive prints from his paper negatives.

The general term *salted paper print* is used to describe a silver printing-out paper which has been fixed in thiosulfate and which consists of a silver image located in and among the paper fibers. Thiosulfate fixer impart-

ed a reddish-brown image hue, and left non-image areas white. The use of the salted paper printing process grew throughout the 1840s, stimulated by the progress of Talbot and others in techniques for making negatives.

The simple kind of salted paper print produced by soaking writing paper in a sodium chloride solution served photographers well throughout the 1840s. The techniques which evolved for exposing prints during this first decade of photography remained in use throughout the 19th century. Printing was done in a printing frame, an appliance which held the negative and sensitized paper in close contact during exposure. Because so much light was required to expose the prints, it was virtually impossible to produce a print by enlargement. Most 19th-century prints are therefore contact prints. Printing could only be done during daylight hours. Exposure times varied from a few minutes to many hours, depending on the season, weather conditions, and the quality of the negative. It was impossible to print outdoors in cold weather.

In the period 1841-1855, the negative-positive approach to photography typically involved a calotype (paper) negative (left) and a salted paper print (right) made from it.

IMPROVEMENTS IN SALTED PAPERS

The paper used to make salted paper prints was important to the success of the process; a smooth, all-rag paper was preferred. Photographers noticed that the sizing of the paper influenced the appearance of the prints.[1] Starch-sized paper yielded brown tones, while gelatin-sized paper gave more reddish image hues. At first the only sizing present was that employed by the paper-makers, but in the early 1850s photographers began to apply extra sizing to increase the density or "brilliance" of the image. Soaking paper in a salt solution was abandoned in favor of combined salting-sizing solutions applied to one side of the paper only.

Many substances were used as sizing materials in the combined salting-sizing approach, including starch, gelatin, casein, serum of milk (whey), and Irish moss (carrageenin).[2] The amount of sizing applied was not enough to form a separate layer of material on the print surface, and prints therefore retained the surface character of the paper itself, and a matte appearance. Because a variety of factors can influence image character, it is not possible to tell visually what type of applied sizing might be present on a salted paper print. However, most salted paper prints made after the early 1850s had applied sizing of some kind.

The salted paper process was used to make prints from both paper negatives and glass negatives. Prints made from paper negatives often have images with a grainy, slightly mottled quality due to the texture of the paper support of the negative. Paper negatives were used exclusively until the late 1840s, and were in limited use until the early 1860s. The term *calotype*, a name given by Talbot in 1841 to his paper negative process, is properly used only in reference to a paper negative or to a print made from a paper negative, and should not be used to refer to salted paper prints in general. In a salted paper print made from a negative on glass, image detail is sharp and crisp with flat tonal areas that are not mottled.

THE ALBUMEN PRINT: 1850-1895

Out of the ceaseless experimentation that characterized the first decades of photography came another printing material, similar in many respects to salted paper, but with a different sort of applied sizing—hen's egg white. This most important print material of the 19th century, the *albumen print*, was the discovery of a French photographer, Louis Desire Blanquart Evrard, and was first announced by him on May 27, 1850.

PREPARATION OF ALBUMEN PAPER

Albumen was prepared by beating salted egg white to a froth, then allowing it to settle back into liquid form. It was applied to the paper by a floating process in which individual sheets were carefully rested on the surface of the solution, then gently lifted off and hung vertically to dry.[3] Albumen was fundamentally superior to more dilute salting-sizing materials because it created an entirely separate layer in which to form the silver image; this made possible much greater density and contrast in the print. The albumen surface was glossy, and its image hues could be altered to a characteristic range of colors.

These were formidable advantages, and the albumen print process became very popular. By 1855 the majority of photographers had adopted it, and salted paper became less common although it did not entirely disappear.

The *albumen print* process dominated photographic practice from 1855-1895. This albumen print was made from a negative produced by a No. 1 KODAK Camera in the early 1890s.

IMP/GEH

With the adoption of albumen paper as the dominant print material, salted paper prints came to be referred to as "plain" paper prints. The actual "manipulations" of albumen paper did not differ significantly from those used for salted papers. In order to be used, albumenized sheets were rendered light-sensitive by being floated albumen side down in a tray of 10% silver nitrate solution. Because the sensitized paper did not keep well, sensitizing, printing, and processing were usually done on the same day.

GOLD TONING

At about the same time as the introduction of albumen paper, there was a new development in the processing of all kinds of silver printing papers. *Gold toning*, in which the silver image was partially converted to gold by treatment in a solution containing gold chloride, came into use. Gold toning originated in 1841 as an improvement in the daguerreotype process, and was first applied to paper prints in 1847.[4] It changed the image hue on a silver printing-out paper

from reddish-brown to purple, and improved the stability of the silver image. Many photographers found the brick-red color of the untoned albumen print to be unattractive, but were pleased by the rich purple hues of the gold-toned print. Except for some very early examples, virtually all albumen prints were gold-toned. The exact color of gold-toned albumen prints varies from warm purplish-brown to blue-black, depending on the toner formula, time of toning, and a number of factors in the preparation and exposure of the albumen paper. The sequence of steps in processing an albumen print included washing, toning, fixing, and final washing.

The growth of the negative/positive system of photography was rapid during the 1850s because of the discovery of the *wet collodion* process for making negatives. So-called "wet-plate" negatives on glass supports displaced daguerreotypy as the dominant portrait medium primarily because they made it easy to obtain duplicate images. It is easy to understand the rapid acceptance which albumen papers gained during the middle and late 1850s. A glossy-surfaced print medium was something of a novelty. An albumen print made from a glass negative had deep, rich tones and crisp detail, and embodied many qualities unique to photography. The "wet-plate" negative and albumen print combination remained in use from 1855 to about 1880, when the *gelatin dry-plate* negative process became popular. The simplicity and convenience of gelatin dry plates made photography more available to non-professionals, and led to increased sales of albumen paper.

SILVER PRINTS FROM DEVELOPING-OUT PROCESSES: 1840–1885

From the 1840s on, techniques to make positive prints by development were available but infrequently used. Contrast was difficult to control with hand-coated developing-out papers, and the neutral black image color of developed prints was unfamiliar to the public. The overwhelming majority of photographic prints made during the 19th century were produced on silver printing-out papers, in which the image was entirely created by exposure to sunlight or daylight. The nature of this process imparted warm brown and purple image colors. This helped to create the pervasive cultural convention that warm image hues are suggestive of the 19th century, or at least of times past.

Photographic negatives cannot be made by a printing-out process because too little light is available in the camera and exposure times would be impossibly long. For most of the 19th century, there existed a dichotomy in silver imaging systems: negatives were produced by development and prints were made by printing-out. There were, however, a few cases in which prints were made by development. Sometimes a print was needed when the weather was unsuitable for exposing printing-out papers, or occasionally a photographer chose developing-out papers because of their increased image stability.[5]

Crayon portraits were enlargements produced by a developing-out process and finished with applied pastels or charcoal. Such prints were often life-size and were made from the 1860s up to the early 20th century.

Constance McCabe

The largest class of prints made by development during that period were enlargements called "crayon portraits," in which a weak photographic image was used as the basis for extensive handwork with charcoal or pastels.[6] They were made from the 1860s through the turn of the 20th century. Both printed-out and developed-out images were used as a basis for applied coloring, but the life-sized crayon portraits usually employed a neutral black, developed-out image on a matte-surfaced paper as the underlying photographic "sketch." On

the whole, however, few developed-out prints were made from 1840 to 1885.

IMPROVEMENTS IN ALBUMEN PAPER: 1860-1885

For some years, photographers coated their own albumen paper; but in the late 1850s, an industry grew up in response to the ever-increasing demand for albumenized paper. One of the most troublesome aspects of making albumen paper was finding a suitable paper base, or "raw stock," which had to be a thin, smooth sheet of exceptional purity and quality. The need for a very thin paper was dictated by the floating method used to coat and sensitize the sheet. If the base paper was too thick, it became too stiff to manipulate when floated on the sensitizing solution. The paper had to be exceptionally pure because silver is very reactive, and impurities in the paper would cause desensitized spots and stains to appear in the print. During the 19th century, only two paper mills in the world, both located in Europe, were able to consistently produce paper good enough to use for albumenizing.[7]

Tinted Albumen Paper

The discovery of new synthetic dyes during the 1860s made possible the tinting of albumen paper. Pink, blue, and violet dyes were added to the albumen before it was coated. The slight highlight coloration that dyes provided lent a pleasing effect and tended to mask the yellowing of the albumen itself. Tinted paper gained popularity during the 1870s, and the bulk of the albumen paper sold after 1880 was tinted. Pink shades were the most popular.

Burnishing

Along with the trend toward tinted albumen paper came the popularity of more glossy print surfaces, especially in commercial portraiture. The smooth surface was attained by applying a second coating of albumen to the paper and by mechanically smoothing the finished print in a roller device known as a "burnisher." Burnishing gained acceptance during the late 1860s and became almost universal by the mid-1870s. Roller presses of various designs were used not only with small portrait formats, but also on album pages prior to binding, and on large prints of all types. When skillfully done, mechanical surface smoothing could produce an extremely high gloss on an albumen print.

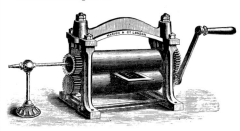

In the mid-1870s, a practice known as "enameling," in which prints were coated with collodion, enjoyed brief popularity.[8] The process was cumbersome, however, and was soon abandoned. Burnishing remained a routine aspect of print finishing until well after albumen paper had been replaced by gelatin and collodion printing-out papers.

Ready-Sensitized Paper

Factory-made albumen paper was not light-sensitive; once sensitized by the photographer, it had to be used almost immediately. Several solutions to the problem of poor keeping quality of sensitized paper were tried. In the early 1870s, the use of citric acid enabled the preparation of sensitized albumen paper with a shelf life of several months. This "ready-sensitized" paper appealed mostly to amateur photographers, whose ranks swelled appreciably during the 1880s. Professional photographers generally continued to sensitize their own paper because it was more economical and gave better results.

NON-SILVER PAPERS: 1860–1900

CARBON PRINTS

One of the major problems with albumen paper and all silver print materials is a tendency to fade and discolor. All through the 19th century interest in finding a more permanent alternative to silver papers ran high. A promising potential source was the family of processes based on the light sensitivity of bichromates, a phenomenon discovered in 1839 by Mungo Ponton. When added to gelatin, gum arabic, or any of a variety of similar substances, bichromates render the coating insoluble upon exposure to light.

In the *carbon print*, a layer of bichromated gelatin containing a pigment (carbon black was one of the first pigments used, hence the name) is exposed under a negative. The gelatin is selectively hardened by light passing through the negative. When the gelatin is gently washed in warm water, the unhardened areas are dissolved away, leaving a positive image of pigmented gelatin. Virtually any pigment could be used. Since inorganic pigments had exceptional stability, the resulting prints were

quite permanent. Sometimes pigments were chosen for their ability to mimic albumen print image colors. After numerous technical difficulties were overcome, the process became practical in the late 1860s, and the pigmented gelatin layers, called "tissues," became commercially available. The beauty and durability of carbon prints was undisputed, but they were too time-consuming and difficult to manipulate to pose a serious challenge to silver papers. Though carbon tissues were sold throughout the balance of the 19th century, carbon prints were never produced in large numbers.

GUM BICHROMATE PRINTS

The *gum bichromate printing process*, based on discoveries made in the early 1850s by the Frenchman Alphonse Poitevin, is a close relative of the carbon print process. Instead of pigmented gelatin, the binder in the gum bichromate process is gum arabic, a viscous substance obtained from the acacia tree. "Gum printing" was almost forgotten until the mid-1890s, when it was adopted by pictorialist photographers who liked its soft effects and the ease with which its images could be manipulated with brushes and handwork.

Being comprised of pigments, the images of gum bichromate prints have excellent stability. Multiple printings (sometimes with different pigment colors) on the same sheet of paper were common, and sometimes a platinotype image was combined with the normal gum bichromate process.

Few gum bichromate prints were made during the 19th century because the process was difficult and popular only among a rather small circle of fine art photographers. For this reason, and because existing gum bichromate prints are now mostly to be found in the larger fine art photography collections, the process does not appear in the *IDENTIFICATION GUIDE* presented in Chapter IV.

PLATINUM PRINTS

An important non-silver print material of the last two decades of the 19th century was the *platinum print* or *platinotype*. The platinotype process is based on the light sensitivity of certain iron salts which, when irradiated, reduce platinum compounds to metallic platinum. The platinotype image consists of finely divided platinum

metal, and is exceptionally stable. The process came into use around 1880 and soon gained many enthusiastic practitioners.

Platinum prints have a matte surface; most have a soft, steely-gray image color, although several variations of the process produced browner image hues. The process was admired for its delicate tonality, and quickly became identified with "artistic" photography. Widespread adoption of the platinotype was initially hampered by the fact that the sensitized paper did not keep well, and by the enormous inflation in the price of platinum during the 1880s and 1890s. The rarity and industrial importance of platinum drove the price so high that the platinotype became too costly for general commercial use.

Platinum papers never threatened the economic domination of silver papers, but during the 1890s silver paper manufacturers tried to copy the platinotype's matte surface and neutral black image color.[9] Many matte-surfaced, silver developing-out and printing-out papers appeared in the mid-1890s. Nearly all used "platino" in their names, and were explicitly compared to platinum prints in trade announcements. This attempt at imitation was even more significant for silver printing-out papers than for silver developing-out papers, because it led to the marketing of what was to become the most popular print material from 1895 to 1905—matte collodion printing-out papers (see later in this chapter).

A matte surface and soft, gray-black color are characteristics of the *platinotype* process. Produced in moderately large numbers in the last two decades of the 19th century, platinotypes show little tendency to fade.

James M. Reilly

CYANOTYPES

The *cyanotype*, or "blueprint" process, was another of Sir John Herschel's contributions to photography. Although the process dates from the 1840s, it was used rather infrequently until the 1890s. Like the platinotype, the cyanotype has a matte print surface and is based on the light sensitivity of iron salts. The cyanotype image is composed of a mixture of ferric ferrocyanide and ferrous ferricyanide, iron complexes respectively known as "Prussian blue" and

TECHNICAL ADVANCES IN SILVER PRINTING PAPERS: 1880–1900

A number of factors combined during the 1880s and 1890s to dramatically increase the total sales of photographic papers. An expanding market provided financial incentives for technical innovations and accelerated the evolution of print materials. During that period, a series of fundamental technical advances affected all types of silver papers, developing-out and printing-out alike.

Cyanotypes have a blue image color and a matte print surface. The process was used successfully both to reproduce architectural drawings and to print pictorial scenes such as this one.

James M. Reilly

"Turnbull's blue" when used as pigments. The image stability of cyanotypes is good, though not as good as that of platinotypes. Cyanotypes fade when exposed to light, but the lost image density is regained in large measure during storage in the dark.

Its blue image color kept the cyanotype from finding wide acceptance as a photographic print material. Cyanotypes were somewhat popular during the 1890s and the first decade of the 20th century, mostly with amateur photographers drawn by their low cost and simple processing. As a photographic print material, the cyanotype did not essentially differ from the blueprint material used to reproduce technical drawings and architectural plans. Cyanotypes were commonly used to make photograms of leaves and plants, and many charming examples created by schoolchildren survive.

BARYTAPAPER

One of these advances was the use of a preparatory coating of gelatin containing a white pigment prior to the application of whatever sensitized coatings were to follow. Around 1880, after several decades of experimentation, the combination of gelatin and the white pigment barium sulfate emerged as the most satisfactory substratum for photographic papers. The common name for barium sulfate was *baryta*, and paper with a gelatin/barium sulfate surface preparation was known as "barytapaper."[10] The baryta layer provided extra brilliance and contrast to prints, and acted as an insulating layer between the sensitized coating and any reactive impurities in the paper fibers below. The baryta coating allowed for greater control over the surface character of the print materials. Unlike paper itself, the baryta coating could be smoothed, roughened, or impressed with a texture. When the sensitized coating was applied, it took on the surface character of the baryta coating.

CONTINUOUS-ROLL COATING

Another fundamental advance was the development of continuous-roll coating machinery for photographic papers. Albumen paper had been coated by hand, one sheet at a time, but the papers introduced in the 1880s—bromide developing-out paper as well as gelatin and collodion printing-out papers—were coated by machine in continuous rolls. Both the baryta substratum and the sensitized coatings were applied in this fashion. Machine-coating lowered the cost of the newer papers and improved their quality and consistency.

Perhaps the most significant advances of this period occurred in the sensitized coatings themselves. The essential difference between albumen paper and all the materials which succeeded it was that the newer papers received a truly sensitized coating consisting of a combination of the binder (gelatin or collodion) and light-sensitive silver salts. Such papers were known as *emulsion* papers to distinguish them from the earlier materials which were first coated with a salting-sizing solution, then sensitized with silver nitrate in a separate step.

With the appearance of sensitized emulsions, barytapaper, and machine coating, modern photographic print materials had arrived. The technology of silver photographic papers today is not fundamentally different from that of the 1890s.

PRINTING-OUT PAPERS AND THE DECLINE OF ALBUMEN: 1885–1900

The pre-eminence of albumen paper above all other photographic printing papers lasted for 40 years, from 1855 to 1895. The enduring popularity of albumen paper was mostly based on its use by portrait photographers and publishers of stereo and topographical views. Albumen paper was relatively inexpensive. Its surface character could be modified from semi-matte to very glossy, and its image quality was very good. Once printing-out papers with comparable image quality became available, however, the deficiencies of albumen paper were

more apparent and it was abandoned in favor of the newer materials.

It may seem surprising that albumen paper was replaced by other printing-out papers and not by the bromide developing-out papers which had become commercially available in the mid-1880s. Bromide papers only became popular much later, when their fast speed was indispensable for making enlargements from small-camera negatives. Taste, tradition, and working methods were all geared to printing-out papers; and many photographers found the great sensitivity of bromide papers more annoying than beneficial.

The gelatin and collodion printing-out papers were much more of a threat to albumen paper. They were coated at the factory with a sensitized emulsion, and therefore did not need to be sensitized by the photographer. They were offered in a wide range of surfaces, image colors, and contrasts. Their image stability was superior: gelatin and collodion papers did not share albumen paper's tendency to yellow in highlight areas, and platinum toning gave excellent image stability to matte collodion papers (see Chapter III). After professional photographers began to abandon albumen paper in the 1890s, it suffered a long decline, but was manufactured as late as the 1920s.

BROMIDE DEVELOPING-OUT PAPER: 1885-1900

During the mid-1880s, a new type of developing-out print appeared, known as *bromide developing-out paper*. It contained a sensitized emulsion similar to the new silver-halide in gelatin emulsions used in the gelatin dry-plate negative process. Steady improvements in gelatin emulsion technology through the 1870s made dry plates quite reliable, and transformed the making of negatives. The application of the very sensitive silver bromide gelatin emulsions to paper prints was a logical extension of the new technology.[11] The earliest bromide developing-out papers (ca. 1885–1895) had no baryta coatings, and were chiefly used to make enlargements and reproduce documents. Subsequently, all but a few specialized grades had baryta coatings, and the paper was offered in both matte and glossy surfaces. Al-

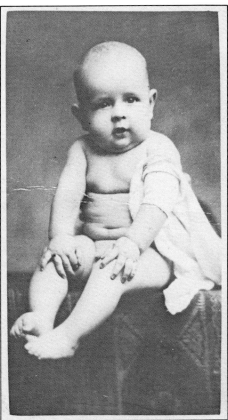

A somewhat faded (but still striking) example of a print on *bromide developing-out paper,* circa 1900. The original neutral black color of this print has given way to brownish-black due to oxidation of the silver image.

James M. Reilly

COLLODION PRINTING-OUT PAPERS

Collodion is a viscous fluid obtained when pyroxylin (cellulose nitrate) is dissolved in a mixture of alcohol and ether. It made its debut in photography as the binder for the silver salts in the wet collodion negative process, discovered by Frederick Scott Archer in 1851. Collodion was also used as the binder in the ambrotype

This early Kodak snapshot was printed on *glossy collodion printing-out paper.* Note the shadow of the photographer in the foreground of the picture.

James M. Reilly

though bromide paper was a commercial success during the 19th century, its use was largely restricted to amateurs and to firms which made a specialty of enlargements. The image color of bromide developing-out paper was neutral black, and its image stability was superior to that of albumen paper.

EMULSION-TYPE PRINTING-OUT PAPERS: 1885-1900

Gelatin and collodion printing-out papers replaced albumen paper as the dominant photographic printing material, and were used from the late 1880s to the late 1920s. They are among the least known of the major silver print materials. Similar in many ways, they differed in one vital respect: the transparent layer in which the light-sensitive silver salts were suspended was gelatin in one case and collodion (a form of cellulose nitrate) in the other. Both materials were of the printing-out type, which meant that the image was created entirely by exposure to light as it was with albumen and salted papers. Despite being printing-out papers, they were distinctly modern in employing sensitized emulsions coated on barytapaper in continuous rolls.

and tintype processes. Experiments with collodion as the carrier for the silver salts in paper prints began as early as 1861, but problems were encountered with poor keeping properties in the sensitized paper and lack of adhesion between the collodion and the paper support. The latter difficulty was overcome through the use of papers with a preparatory coating similar to baryta, and experiments with collodion papers played a significant role in the development of baryta coating technology. By 1867, a hand-coated collodion printing-out paper was commercially available, but not until the late 1880s did it begin to gain popularity.[12]

Collodion printing-out papers were coated on barytapaper and contained a sensitized emulsion of silver chloride stabilized by the presence of citric acid. All of the emulsion type printing-out papers of the 1880s made use of the stabilizing properties of citric acid, the same ingredient which had made "ready-sensitized" albumen papers possible. The shelf life of emulsion printing-out papers (both collodion and gelatin) was approximately one year under favorable climatic conditions.

The first collodion printing-out papers to go into large-scale production were very glossy to appeal to the prevailing taste of the 1880s for glossy commercial portraiture. A skillful operator could burnish a collodion paper to a degree of smoothness equal to that of the glossiest modern resin-coated papers. Collodion does not absorb water or swell when wetted. This led to severe curling problems during processing and gave collodion papers a reputation for being difficult to work with. This problem was moderated by the addition of plasticizers to the collodion. Glossy collodion papers closely resembled glossy gelatin printing-out papers in surface character and image color, and the processing and finishing techniques used for the two types of papers were essentially the same. Gold toning was used with both, and produced a variety of image hues from reddish-brown to purple.

Glossy collodion papers were the first emulsion type printing-out paper to be marketed. They enjoyed early success, only to lose ground to glossy gelatin printing-out papers in the early 1890s.

MATTE COLLODION PRINTING-OUT PAPERS

In the mid-1890s changing tastes prompted the introduction of *matte collodion printing-out paper*. This material was sold under names which included the word "platino," signifying a conscious attempt to imitate the qualities of the platinotypes. The image color of printing-out papers was strongly dependent on the type of toning treatment used. At first, gold toners which gave nearly black tones, were recommended. Soon, however, a combination of gold toning followed by platinum toning became standard for the processing of matte collodion printing-out papers. This treatment partially converted the image silver to both gold and platinum. The image color was a warm olive-black, tending to bluer shades when the gold toning was strong, and to browner shades when the gold toning was minimal.

Matte collodion paper created an immediate sensation, and during the later 1890s it came to dominate commercial practice almost as completely as albumen paper had during the 1870s.[13] Its position as the material of choice for portrait photographs lasted until about 1910, when it was supplanted by contact-speed developing-out papers. The image quality of matte collodion printing-out papers was exceptional. Because of the dual toning treatment, matte collodion papers possessed a very high degree of image stability, and most prints are even now in quite good condition. Yet it is a great irony that this paper appeared at the very time when photographic artists were most disdainful of the materials used by professional photographers and were least disposed to "straight" photography.

With delicate tonality and a high degree of permanence, this portrait from the late 1890s owes its enduring beauty to *matte collodion printing-out paper* toned with gold and platinum.

James M. Reilly

12

GELATIN PRINTING-OUT PAPERS

Gelatin printing-out papers made use of the same type of silver chloride sensitized emulsion as collodion papers, with the important difference that gelatin and not collodion was the binder for the sensitive salts. The experience gained from the production of bromide developing-out papers in the 1880s was directly applicable to

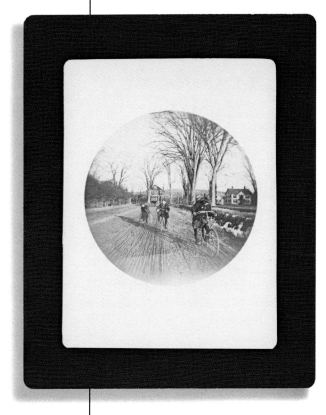

Photography and bicycling were popular pastimes during the 1890s. This Kodak snapshot was printed on *gelatin printing-out paper*.

James M. Reilly

gelatin printing-out papers, since both were machine-coated on baryta stock and differed only in the photographic properties of the emulsion.

The first gelatin printing-out papers appeared in the late 1880s and had a glossy surface. They were customarily toned with gold and displayed purple-brown image hues generally similar to those of albumen paper and glossy collodion printing-out paper. An early problem with the material was the delicacy of the gelatin emulsion during processing, when the swollen gelatin was easily scratched and abraded. The addition of gelatin hardeners largely overcame this problem.

Gelatin printing-out papers outsold collodion papers in the early 1890s when glossy papers were in fashion, and the two materials were virtually indistinguishable. But gelatin print-

ing-out papers simply could not mimic the surface quality, image colors, and overall effect of matte collodion papers. The latter captured a large market share in the mid-1890s at the expense of both albumen paper and glossy gelatin printing-out papers. Matte gelatin papers were produced, but tended to be more matte-surfaced than their collodion counterparts because their surface effects were obtained by adding "matting agents" such as rice starch and shellac to the gelatin emulsion.

CONTACT-SPEED DEVELOPING-OUT PAPERS: LATE 1890s

The advantages of development over the printing-out approach were formidable, and by 1905 the combined sales of developing-out papers finally exceeded those of printing-out papers. Commercial users liked developing-out papers because of their lower cost (no precious metal toning was required) and faster, more reliable production. Amateurs were attracted to developing-out papers because they did not need to be daylight exposed.

During the late 1890s, several varieties of slow-speed developing-out papers were introduced, and appealed to a much wider public than bromide papers had just a few years before.[14] Slow, contact-speed developing-out papers became known as "gaslight" papers because they could be both exposed and processed indoors by the light of gas illuminators. To expose the paper, the gas flame was turned up high and the printing frame was held close to the light; for processing, the flame was turned low and the trays placed a few feet from the lamp. The image colors of the slow developing-out papers varied from warm, greenish-black to a cold blue-black. All of the slow developing-out papers employed a silver chloride or silver chloro-bromide gelatin emulsion coated on barytapaper. Both smooth and glossy surfaces were offered. Sales of slow developing-out papers increased dramatically in the last three or four years of the 19th century, led by an ever-increasing number of amateurs.

13

Chapter II:

THE COMPONENT MATERIALS OF 19TH-CENTURY PRINTS AND THEIR FORMS OF DETERIORATION

The structures and component materials of 19th-century photographic prints are vulnerable to a variety of forms of deterioration. This chapter presents a general discussion of those structures and materials; the next chapter addresses the specific stability problems of individual processes. The extreme diversity of types of 19th-century prints should be apparent even from the brief history in the previous chapter. In the face of this diversity, a general knowledge of the component substances of prints, their behavior during long-term keeping, and especially of the problems caused by their laminate structures will help to establish appropriate handling procedures and environmental keeping conditions.

In assessing stability problems it is useful to consider photographic print

five of these components, but most do. In the discussion that follows, each component is defined and the properties of substances used in 19th-century prints are examined.

FINAL IMAGE MATERIALS

The image in every photograph is created by something that absorbs or scatters light. The substance which actually comprises the image in the finished, processed photograph is known as the *final image material*. In the case of prints, the final image material selectively absorbs light that would otherwise be reflected from the paper support. The final image material in most 19th-century prints is finely divided metallic silver, but a number of other substances can also be found.

Both the photographic print and its mount can be composed of multiple layers with each layer responding to environmental conditions in different ways. This sketch shows the various layers present in a mounted gelatin printing-out paper print.

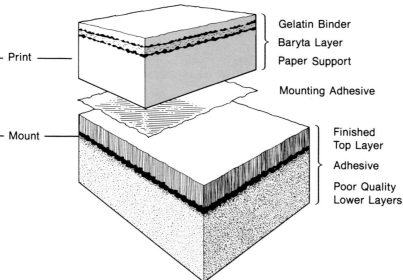

Print —
- Gelatin Binder
- Baryta Layer
- Paper Support

Mounting Adhesive

Mount —
- Finished Top Layer
- Adhesive
- Poor Quality Lower Layers

materials in the light of a structural analysis in which the following "generic" components appear:

1. Final image material
2. Binder
3. Support
4. Secondary support
5. Surface treatments and adhesives

Not all 19th-century prints have all

In a real sense the final image material is the most important part of a print because it physically embodies the pictorial information. If nothing else were known about a photograph except the nature of its final image material, a general assessment of its relative permanence and many of its specific stability problems could still be made. For example, knowing that

14

an image consists wholly or partially of metallic platinum would suggest that it would be quite resistant to fading, because platinum is a very stable chemical substance which does not easily oxidize or tarnish. On the other hand, knowing that part of the image in a print is applied watercolor might cause concern about light damage to its delicate pigments.

METALLIC SILVER

By far the most important final image material found in 19th-century photographs is *metallic silver*. All of the 19th-century print processes based on the light sensitivity of silver compounds formed images made of silver metal. The differences in appearance and variations in relative permanence among silver images depend on the *physical form* of the silver in the image deposit. An untoned salted paper print, for example, has a very reddish image color, while a contact-speed developing-out paper has a nearly neutral black image hue, even though both images consist only of metallic silver. Under adverse environmental conditions, the salted paper print will fade and lose highlight detail far more rapidly than the developed-out print.[15] The reasons for this have to do with the physical form of the silver image rather than any profound chemical differences. All silver images are made up of discrete particles so small that an electron microscope is needed to resolve them. The color and durability of silver images depend in a complex way on the exact size and shape of these particles, and on how closely they are packed together.[16]

Generally speaking, relatively small silver particles give warm image colors—yellows, reds and browns—while relatively large particles create black or nearly neutral images. Particle shape "fine-tunes" the effects of particle size. Highly elongated or irregular silver particles tend to make an image more neutral black than the same amount of silver in spherical particles. A third influence on image color is the closeness of the particles to each other. A compact group of particles interact with light as if they were a single, larger particle, and therefore produce a more neutral image. The nuances of image color among photographs with silver as the final image material stem from the interplay of these submicroscopic structural features.

Forms of Silver in 19th-Century Prints

The microstructure of silver images, so crucial to their color and relative resistance to deterioration, originates during the initial formation of the image. There are three basic structural forms in which silver images occur: photolytic silver, physically developed silver, and filamentary silver.

In all of the printing-out processes—salted paper prints, albumen prints, and gelatin and collodion printing-out papers—the image deposit is composed of *photolytic silver*. "Photolytic" literally means "separated by light." Of the three structural types of silver images, photolytic silver has the smallest particle size and produces red or brown image colors. Photolytic silver particles are roughly spherical. The images they produce have smaller and fewer particles in highlight areas than in shadow areas because the particle size is directly proportional to the amount of light received during exposure.

In a silver image formed by the use of a developing solution after a brief exposure to light, the physical form of the silver particles is determined by the nature of the developer.[17] However, development always creates larger particles than occur in photolytic silver. Developed-out images have near-neutral image colors, with individual particles which are often slightly larger in highlight than in shadow areas. The higher density of the shadow areas is caused by more, not larger, particles.

Certain developers produce round particles of a size up to several hundred times larger than photolytic silver particles. Such image deposits are known as *physically developed silver* and can be found in calotype negatives and in the wet collodion family of processes, including ambrotypes and tintypes. The developing solutions which produce physically developed silver were mostly used from 1840 to 1880, when few prints were done by development processes. Physically developed silver is therefore somewhat rare in 19th-century prints.

More common is *filamentary silver*, the form which occurs in the developing-out papers popular from the end of the 19th century to the present.

15

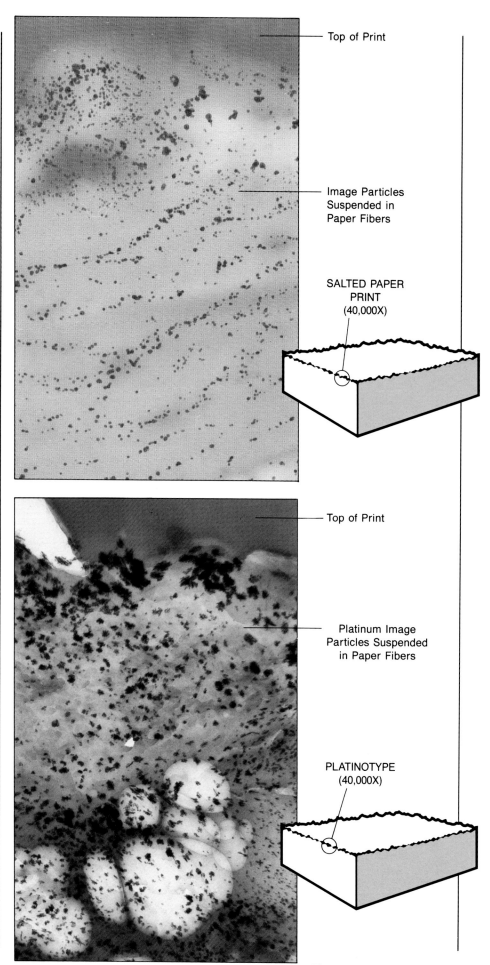

Top of Print

Image Particles
Suspended in
Paper Fibers

SALTED PAPER
PRINT
(40,000X)

Top of Print

Platinum Image
Particles Suspended
in Paper Fibers

PLATINOTYPE
(40,000X)

The individual image particles of the various 19th-century photographic print processes are so small that transmission electron microscopy is necessary to see them. These cross-sectional views depict a small area (usually near the uppermost surface) of each type of print.

Microscopy by T. Van Dam,
Research Laboratories,
Eastman Kodak Company

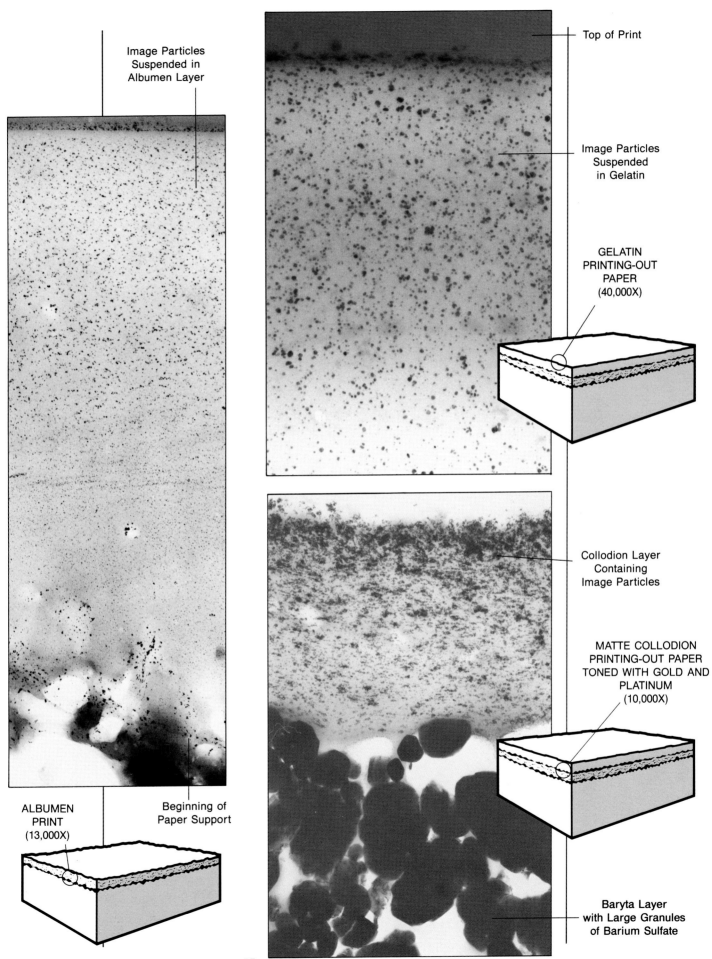

Image Particles
Suspended in
Albumen Layer

Top of Print

Image Particles
Suspended
in Gelatin

GELATIN
PRINTING-OUT
PAPER
(40,000X)

Collodion Layer
Containing
Image Particles

MATTE COLLODION
PRINTING-OUT PAPER
TONED WITH GOLD AND
PLATINUM
(10,000X)

ALBUMEN
PRINT
(13,000X)

Beginning of
Paper Support

Baryta Layer
with Large Granules
of Barium Sulfate

17

The image structure of a 19th-century albumen print consists of small, nearly round particles of silver, as shown in this cross-section transmission electron micrograph at 40,000X. Compare the size and shape of the albumen print particles with those of the contemporary black-and-white print shown below.

Microscopy by T. Van Dam, Research Laboratories, Eastman Kodak Company

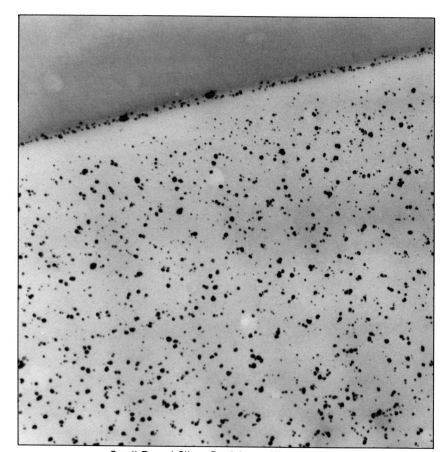

Small Round Silver Particles—Albumen Print

The image structure of a modern gelatin developing-out print is comprised of isolated clumps of filamentary silver, as shown in this electron micrograph at 40,000X. The size and filamentary character of the silver clumps vary according to the emulsion-making technique and the developer used. Gelatin developing-out papers in the 19th century probably had a more filamentary structure than this modern paper because of the developer solutions in use at that time.

Research Laboratories, Eastman Kodak Company

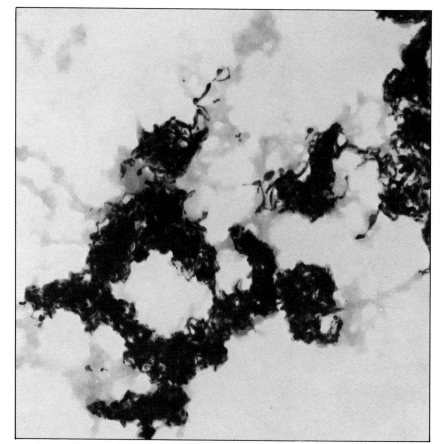

Large Clumps of Filamentary Silver—Contemporary Black-and-White Print

Along with the new bromide, chloride and chloro-bromide papers came new developing agents which deposited silver in the form of slender, twisted strands—hence the term "filamentary." A typical "particle" of filamentary silver consists of a bundle of intertwined filaments that are huge in comparison with the small spheres of photolytic silver. The large size and irregular, disordered structure of the filament bundles are ideal for absorbing light. They produce a neutral black image color.

DETERIORATION MECHANISMS FOR SILVER IMAGES

The two basic mechanisms by which silver images deteriorate are sulfiding and oxidative-reductive deterioration. One need not be a chemist to understand these mechanisms and take appropriate measures to retard or prevent them.

Sulfiding Deterioration of Silver Images

Silver has a strong tendency to react irreversibly with sulfur to form the

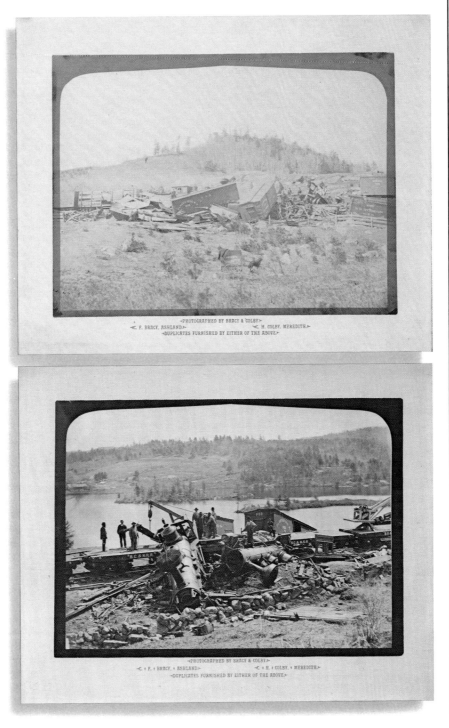

These two albumen prints have both suffered from the effects of oxidative image deterioration caused by humid air and poor quality mount boards. The additional highlight yellowing, fading, and change in image color seen in the print on top are due to inadequate washing when the print was originally processed.

James M. Reilly

very stable substance silver sulfide. The general type of deterioration resulting from this reaction is called *sulfiding*. The tarnish on silver household objects is the result of the formation of a thin film of silver sulfide due to small amounts of sulfiding gases in the atmosphere. Daguerreotype plates tarnish similarly. Sulfiding on paper prints can be due to either atmospheric sources of sulfur or, more commonly, sources within the print itself. Hydrogen sulfide and other sulfiding gases in the atmosphere do not usually occur in high enough concentrations to damage severely photographic prints. They act only as a contributing factor in the more significant damage done by oxidative-reductive deterioration. In some localized regions, however, the concentration of sulfiding gases may be high enough to cause serious damage.

A more extensive set of preservation problems arises from a source of sulfur intrinsic to prints—residual processing chemicals. Sodium thiosulfate, the compound used to fix silver images, is a sulfur compound which over time (though quite rapidly in the presence of moisture) breaks down and releases reactive sulfur to attack the silver image. All of the thiosulfate used in fixing must be removed by thorough washing in water if sulfiding deterioration is to be avoided. Thiosulfate is tenaciously retained by paper fibers and baryta coatings, so that prints with relatively thick paper supports or baryta layers (such as gelatin and collodion printing-out papers, and all of the gelatin developing-out papers) have more problems due to retained thiosulfate than albumen prints do. The thin paper support and lack of a baryta layer in albumen prints allow for effective washing in a relatively short time.[18]

The observable symptoms of sulfiding deterioration due to atmospheric sources of sulfur or retained thiosulfate differ somewhat for photolytic silver and filamentary silver. In filamentary silver images, the highlights are attacked first, turning yellow, fading and losing detail until the entire image is affected. The non-image areas for the most part remain white. Such deterioration can be rapid if large amounts of thiosulfate are present. It should be noted that the symptoms of sulfiding for filamentary images quite closely resemble those of oxidative-

reductive deterioration (see p. 21), so that it is not possible to visually diagnose the cause as sulfiding.

For photolytic silver images, the consequences of sulfiding are more distinctive and have several stages. The highlights are attacked first, becoming yellow and fading. The middletone and shadow areas become more neutral in hue before fading to a yellow or yellow-green color[19]. The intermediate blackening of the image is caused by a partial conversion of the photolytic silver image particles to silver sulfide. This actually enlarges them, and the larger, partially sulfided particles have new absorption characteristics and appear more neutral.

A photolytic silver image undergoing oxidative-reductive deterioration becomes progressively redder or yellower, with no intermediate blackening stage. This makes the visual identification of sulfiding deterioration in printing-out papers more certain than is possible with developing-out papers.

The second kind of sulfiding deterioration, due to improper original processing of silver prints, is caused by the use of exhausted fixing baths. The fixing action of thiosulfates depends on the fact that they form a series of complexes with silver ions. The nature of these complexes is determined by how much thiosulfate is available, and an excess is needed for the most freely soluble complex to be formed. Without enough thiosulfate, as in an exhausted fixing bath, the less soluble complexes predominate and remain in the print despite all attempts to remove them by washing in water. This has consequences for image stability quite different from those caused by residual thiosulfate alone. Most importantly, the non-image areas of prints fixed in exhausted fixer gradually become stained with a yellowish-brown deposit of silver sulfide, the ultimate product of the decomposition of silver thiosulfates. The presence of silver thiosulfate in image areas also leads to the formation of silver sulfide composed of silver from both the image itself and the thiosulfate. The net result is yellowing and fading; but because of the additional silver sulfide formation, somewhat more highlight density and detail are preserved than would be if the image were attacked by thiosulfate

Silver mirroring is a common symptom of oxidative-reductive deterioration in silver images. It appears as a bluish metallic sheen in dark areas and is most readily visible when a light source is reflected off the print surface at a low angle (right).

James M. Reilly

alone. For all types of silver images, the staining effect of residual silver thiosulfate is obvious; but blackening and staining are good indications of retained silver thiosulfates in photolytic (printed-out) silver images.[20]

Oxidative-Reductive Deterioration of Silver Images

The most important deterioration mechanism for silver images is *oxidative-reductive deterioration*,[21] which occurs when silver is attacked by any of a wide variety of oxidants that convert metallic silver atoms to the highly reactive, highly mobile, colorless species known as *silver ions*. Unlike sulfiding deterioration, which can be observed as tarnish on silver spoons and other silver objects, oxidation only becomes a serious problem when silver is in the form of very small particles, as it is in photographs. This is because oxidation occurs at the surface of silver, and the small particles of photographic images have enormously more surface area relative to their total mass than do larger silver objects. The smaller the individual particles of a photographic image, the more rapidly they will be affected by oxidative-reductive deterioration. This is the primary reason why filamentary silver images have good inherent resistance to fading, and photolytic silver images do not. The fading of silver images which has plagued photography from its earliest days is mostly a consequence of oxidative-reductive deterioration.

The term "oxidative-reductive deterioration" is used rather than "oxidation" because this form of deterioration is a continuing cycle of chemical changes involving oxidation of silver to silver ions, migration away from the original particle site, and *reduction* back to metallic, elemental silver.[22] Oxidation damages the image because silver ions and whatever silver compounds may form are colorless and unable to contribute to the image by absorbing light. The reduction step of the cycle, the speed and extent of which depend on a number of factors, is sometimes beneficial because it returns the silver to the metallic state in which it can again absorb light and contribute to the image. But the metallic silver formed during reduction is deposited in a new location and in a different physical form than that of the original image. The net result of oxidative-reductive deterioration is a decrease in the total amount of silver in the metallic state and, more importantly, a physical redistribution and rearrangement of the image silver. Because the physical form of the silver determines its color and density, oxidative-reductive deterioration causes fading and shifts in image hue.

Oxidative-reductive deterioration involves a complex and difficult set of chemical reactions. Many oxidants can cause deterioration, and they need only be present in minute quantities to be effective. Oxidant gases are generated by industrial pollution, automobiles, and a host of other processes and materials, including heavy electrical machinery, oil-base paints, and poor quality cardboard.[23] One needs to be aware of the potential sources of oxidants, but it is impossible to detect their presence or deal with them as individual chemical species. To cope with oxidative-reductive deterioration—the most serious long-term threat to the survival of silver images—a method is needed to retard oxidation, regardless of the specific oxidant involved.

Fortunately, the rate of oxidative-reductive deterioration can be retarded by controlling relative humidity (RH). Moisture plays a central role in the oxidation of silver images. Under dry conditions little or no oxidation takes place; under very moist conditions the rate of oxidation is maximized. In terms of the silver image alone, the best storage conditions for photographs would be arid. However, some moisture is needed to prevent paper, albumen, and gelatin from becoming too brittle. The optimum relative humidity for a photographic collection should therefore be between 30 and 40%. (Caution: These conditions may not be best for leather or other types of objects. See Chapter VI.) Temperature influences the rate of oxidative-reductive deterioration—nearly all chemical reactions are faster at higher temperatures—but the decisive factor is relative humidity. Sustained high relative humidity is devastating to silver images, as shown by the generally poor condition of photographs stored in tropical regions.

Effects of Oxidative-Reductive Deterioration

The visual effects of oxidative-reductive deterioration vary depending on the type of silver image affected. For printed-out (photolytic silver) images, the outstanding changes include rapid loss of highlight detail, overall fading, and a change of image color toward warmer (redder and yellower) hues.[20] The highlights of photolytic silver images have smaller and fewer particles than the shadows, making their lighter image tones particularly vulnerable to oxidative attack. The loss of the lighter tones robs photographic prints of their three-dimensionality by removing, for example, the delicate shadings found in

faces and in the folds of light clothing. The loss of highlight detail occurs in all silver images, but is especially acute in photolytic silver images, whose generally small particle size also makes them fade faster in middletones and shadow areas. In addition, the photolytic particle size is within a range in which minor changes in size will alter image hue.

The situation is better with filamentary silver images. The ultimate consequences of oxidative-reductive deterioration in such images will be fading, loss of highlight detail, and a change in image hue to yellowish-brown. The images, however, will take much longer to reach such a level of deterioration. Under adverse conditions, there is the same amount of chemical assault on filamentary images as on photolytic images, but filamentary images have more silver and are structurally much better equipped to resist attack. The filament bundles are larger than they need to be to create a black image color. As they deteriorate, individual filaments become shorter and break up into smaller pieces, but the bundle retains its capacity to absorb light. Eventually the filamentary character of the image silver is lost, a significant amount of the image silver migrates away from the bundle, and the remnants of the filaments impart a yellow-brown image color.[24]

In all types of silver images the reduction of migrating silver ions can also lead to changes in the appearance of the image. The formation of silver "mirrors," a bluish metallic sheen in shadow areas, is a result of the reduction of silver ions at the very uppermost surface of gelatin, collodion, or albumen[25] layers. Silver mirroring is a symptom of oxidative-reductive deterioration, and can be found in nearly every type of silver photograph with a separate binder layer. It occurs most frequently in glossy developing-out papers, but does not occur in binderless print materials such as salted paper prints.

TONING OF SILVER IMAGES

Nineteenth-century photographic printing made much greater use of precious metal toning—the treatment of the silver image with gold, platinum, or a combination of the two—than does modern printing. Except for some early examples, all of the

printing-out papers used during the 19th century were toned, usually with gold.

A toned silver image undergoes two significant transformations: a change in its composition to a silver-gold or silver-platinum alloy, and a physical change in the size and shape of the image particles. Printing-out papers were toned to improve their appearance by altering their color and to improve their image stability. During toning, some of the silver atoms are replaced with atoms of gold or platinum. The gold does not form a "skin" on the surface of the silver particle, but actually becomes distributed within the crystalline structure of the silver. In the process, the particles become somewhat smaller and are distorted from their original shape.[15]

Gold-silver and gold-platinum-silver alloys have different light absorption characteristics than pure silver and are far more resistant to oxidation. The change in image color which results from toning is a function of both the alteration of particle shape and its composition. Toning a neutral black, filamentary silver image with gold or platinum protects it from oxidation but does not alter its color. Photolytic silver, however, is dramatically altered in color when toning treatments affect its particle size and composition. The amount of color change and degree of protection against oxidation depend on how much silver has been replaced by the other metals. Gold toning of photolytic silver images tends to make them colder and more purple in image hue, transforming the warm red color of the pure silver image to brown, purple or even blue-black. Platinum toning, which was not extensively practiced until the 1890s, turns a photolytic silver image brown. Platinum

toning was most often done in combination with gold toning, yielding nearly neutral tones.

Gold toning by itself protects photolytic silver images to some degree, but does not make them stable. Gold-toned printing-out papers are still less durable than untoned filamentary silver images. But the combination of gold and platinum toning makes photolytic silver more resistant to oxidative attack than untoned filamentary silver. Except for problems with surface abrasion, gold-and-platinum-toned matte collodion printing-out papers survive, for the most part, in excellent condition. Gold-and-platinum-toned prints are also more stable under sulfiding attack. Although they are resistant to sulfiding attack from retained thiosulfate, they become stained in non-image areas when silver thiosulfates are present.

Controlled sulfiding of silver images was also used as a toning treatment for both photolytic and filamentary images. Sulfur toning was widely used during the 1840s to alter the color of salted paper prints. It was claimed that all of the image colors possible with gold toning could be achieved through the controlled sulfiding of the image. Whether or not this was true, it soon became apparent that sulfur-toned salted paper prints were far less stable than their untoned counterparts. It was impossible to limit the sulfiding of photolytic silver images to the precise intermediate state at which a neutral image hue was achieved but no further sulfiding would occur. By 1855 the technique had been repudiated in photographic literature, and gold toning was standard.[26]

When filamentary silver images were produced at the end of the 19th century, sulfur toning enjoyed a re-

Gold toning alters the image color of silver printing-out papers. An untoned print is brick-red, while the color of a toned print (right) is usually purplish-brown. (Examples on gelatin printing-out paper prepared by Dr. Fritz Wentzel).

IMP/GEH

vival—this time with better results. Filamentary silver images are more amenable to sulfur toning than photolytic images. They retain more density and detail with a pleasing brown or "sepia" color, when converted to silver sulfide. By slightly overexposing a print and completely converting the silver to silver sulfide, fully satisfactory and very stable prints can be made on most types of developing-out papers.[27]

the support. Although the particle size in platinotypes affects image color somewhat (brown, blue-black, and neutral black hues are possible), the image color will not change over time due to changes in particle size, shape, or composition.

Platinum is an excellent catalyst for many chemical reactions. Some reactions occur on the surface of platinum which would not otherwise occur, and in which the platinum itself does not take part or become affected. The cat-

This platinotype in its folder illustrates how prints containing platinum can cause the formation of a duplicate transfer image. While the paper cover was closed, its discoloration was catalyzed by the platinum metal, thereby producing the transfer image.

IMP/GEH

METALLIC PLATINUM

Although platinum-toned silver images were more numerous, true platinotypes, in which the final image material consists entirely of metallic platinum, were also made in large numbers during the 19th century. The platinotype's image is in the physical form of irregular, sometimes elongated masses of the same size or a little larger than photolytic silver image particles. The microstructure of the platinotype image is quite different from that of a photolytic silver image toned with platinum because the deposition of the platinum metal occurs under different conditions. The outstanding characteristic of platinum images is their resistance to both oxidative-reductive deterioration and sulfiding. Under normal environmental conditions, the platinum image can be regarded as permanent and unchanging. Preservation difficulties with platinotypes tend to stem from other print components, especially

alytic activity of platinum causes the frequently observed phenomenon of "transfer images." This occurs when a paper or board in contact with a photograph becomes discolored with a brown or yellow stain, which is an exact, positive duplicate of the photographic image. A transfer image can be created by either a pure platinum image or a platinum-toned silver print, and is formed when the discoloration of the paper or board is catalyzed or "speeded up" by contact with the platinum. The transfer image consists of those parts of the paper or board which are in a more advanced state of deterioration than the areas not in contact with the platinum.

Environmental factors which influence the degradation of paper, such as temperature, moisture and air pollution, also influence the rate of the catalytic transfer image phenomenon. Prints in storage should be interleaved or properly housed in sleeves or mats so as not to damage each other in this way. The catalytic activity of platinum can also threaten the paper support of the print by contributing to its embrittlement or discoloration.

COMPLEX IRON SALTS

The final image material of cyanotypes is a mixture of two iron compounds, ferrous ferricyanide and ferric ferrocyanide, both of which are blue. These iron complexes are usually stable under normal environmental conditions, but are subject to photochemical deterioration and lose their color in the presence of alkalies. Exposure to light chemically changes cyanotype images to a colorless form. To some extent the change reverses itself in the dark and the blue color is restored, but the conservator must always seek to limit photochemical deterioration by carefully controlling the illumination of cyanotypes while in storage or on display. Cyanotype images subjected to alkaline conditions fade to a very pale brown and lose almost all detail and density.[28] Cyanotypes should therefore not be treated in alkaline solutions of any kind or be stored in alkaline-buffered paper enclosures.

PIGMENTS AND DYES

As described in the first chapter, a number of 19th-century photographic print processes used pigments or dyes as the final image material. A *pigment* is a solid substance added to another substance to give it color. A *dye*, for the purposes of this discus-

sion, is a synthetic, organic colorant typically added from a solution, and not as a solid. It is impossible to adequately discuss here all of the pigments and dyes used during the 19th century (there is an extensive range of literature on the subject), but a few generalizations can be helpful.

Pigments are typically oxides or salts of transition metals and have excellent stability compared to silver images. Nineteenth-century print processes which used pigments as the final image material included carbon prints, gum bichromate, and a number of related processes. The various pigments used in these prints show small differences in sensitivity to atmospheric pollutants and some differences in stability to light, but essentially all images in which pigment is dispersed in a binder like gelatin or gum arabic have good overall stability.[29]

Synthetic dyes as a group are far less inherently stable than pigments, particularly in response to light. Dyes were used in 19th-century photography in hand-colored prints and transparencies, in tinting albumen and baryta layers, and as an occasional substitute for inorganic pigments in the carbon process. The stability of synthetic dyes varies widely, but most are affected in the dark by temperature, moisture, and pollution.

Minimizing light damage should be the chief concern for images in which dyes or pigments have been used as applied color. Such coloring is com-

Many 19th-century photographic prints contain applied coloring, as in this Japanese albumen print enhanced with watercolors.

IMP/GEH

Hand-coloring of albumen prints with watercolor and (after the mid-1860s) synthetic dyes took several forms. This is a so-called "tissue stereo" which is colored on the back side. By reflected light (top), no color is visible; but when illuminated with transmitted light (bottom), the lifelike coloring is apparent.

IMP/GEH

monly encountered in salted papers and albumen prints, but is less common in gelatin and collodion printing-out papers. Prior to the 1860s, the only colorants used were artist's watercolors. Synthetic dyes, often recognizable by their intensity of color, were used for hand coloring as soon as they became available.

Illumination levels and display times must be carefully controlled when exhibiting images which include either pigments or synthetic dyes as applied color. A watercolor pigment lightly applied to a photographic print does not have the same level of light stability that it has when present in much greater quantity in a gelatin or gum binder. The synthetic dyes extensively used to tint the albumen prior to the coating of albumen paper are so sensitive to light that only prints in albums or those never displayed have kept their full color-

ation.[30] The great dilution of tinting dyes in albumen paper contributed to their poor light stability. The coloration that dye gives an albumen print is a subtle but definite part of the image, and every effort should be made to identify tinted prints and protect them from light damage.

When an overall tint was desired in print materials with a baryta layer, the dye was added to the baryta/gelatin substratum rather than to the gelatin or collodion sensitized emulsion. The light stability of tinted baryta layers was much better than that of tinted albumen layers. Pigments, and to some extent dyes, also served as the final image material in 19th-century photomechanical (printing) processes.

BINDERS

The *binder* is the transparent layer in a photographic material in which the

26

Overall tinting of photographic papers with pink or blue dyes was common with albumen prints and, as these later examples show, with gelatin and collodion printing-out papers. Such strong tints resulted from dyes added to the baryta layer rather than the emulsion.

James M. Reilly

final image material is suspended and protected. Binders play an important role in image formation and in determining such optical properties of prints as surface character, density, and color. Binders also influence the overall stability of prints. The binder material most commonly used in 19th-century print materials was albumen, but collodion and gelatin were also popular. A knowledge of the properties of these important binder materials is helpful in assessing the stability problems of a number of individual print processes.

ALBUMEN

Albumen is the white of a hen's egg, a mixture of proteins with structural properties significantly different from those of gelatin. Both the chemical and physical properties of albumen cause stability problems in photographic prints. From a chemical viewpoint, albumen has a large number of constituent substances and possible deteriorative reactions. Its chemical diversity is to be expected, since albumen supplies most of the proteins and some of the nutrients for a developing chick embryo.

One of the outstanding characteristics of albumen is its tendency to yellow over time.[31] Albumen's chemical makeup includes several sets of constituents which can react with each other to form yellow substances. The deteriorative chemical changes which cause yellowing can also cause

albumen to become fluorescent. The extent to which albumen turns yellow primarily depends on the relative humidity of the storage environment. The tendency of the albumen binder to yellow, together with the extreme sensitivity to moisture of the photolytic silver image, make the strict control of relative humidity doubly essential to the preservation of albumen prints.

Albumen yellowing also occurs from photochemical deterioration due to prolonged exposure to light and from contact with highly lignified, poor quality paper and board. Many albumen prints have been stained and faded by their mounting boards.

The chemical properties of albumen are responsible for another mechanism causing yellowing of the non-image areas of albumen prints. Albumen has a high affinity for silver ions and reacts with them to form a silver-protein compound. Some of the silver associated with albumen during sensitizing is not removed during fixation and remains as colorless silver albumenate. If any source of reactive sulfur is present (such as thiosulfate retained as a result of poor washing), the colorless protein-bound silver will be converted to yellow silver sulfide and cause staining. Albumen is unique among photographic binders in forming this "unfixable" silver-protein compound in all areas of the print after processing.

Very few 19th-century albumen

prints have eluded all of the possible causes of yellow staining and survived with nearly white non-image areas. The yellowing of prints in collections is now so far advanced that in most cases it is difficult to imagine their original appearance.

The structure of protein molecules determines the physical properties of protein layers. Albumen has a different structure from gelatin and does not form a reversible gel. The albumen layer is rendered insoluble in water by the silver sensitizing solution, and the albumen layer is initially a continuous, somewhat flexible coating. But the physical properties of albumen are affected by its moisture content and state of deterioration. Albumen becomes brittle and contracts under dry conditions and softens and swells under moist conditions. Over time, chemical changes occur in albumen which accentuate its brittleness. These changes make it vulnerable to fracturing and cracking, as well as impermeable to water. Dry or deteriorating albumen fractures under applied stress. Fissures and cracks found in albumen layers provide a useful clue for identifying albumen prints.

GELATIN

Gelatin is a commercial product extracted from animal hides, bones and sinews under controlled temperature and pH conditions.[32] Photographic gelatin is a highly purified protein material which is much more homogenous in structure and composition than albumen. Gelatin is fairly stable chemically; most of its stability problems result from its physical properties. It does not share albumen's tendency to yellow from internal causes or albumen's sensitivity to light. Gelatin swells much more than albumen when moist, and contracts and becomes brittle under dry conditions. It becomes liquid at temperatures around 80°F (30°C); at cooler temperatures, it sets to a reversible gel.

Deteriorative changes in gelatin can make it either more brittle, like albumen, or softer, with a greater tendency to swell when moist. This swelling and softening can create a problem when gelatin prints are in contact with plastic sleeves under humid conditions. The softened gelatin adheres to the plastic, especially if the sleeve and print are forced together under pressure. This problem is known as "ferrotyping," and even if the sleeve and gelatin do not adhere, the gelatin's surface character can be permanently modified in the areas of contact. Swelling also allows oxidant gases to diffuse more easily through the gelatin and attack the silver image; this is also a problem with albumen prints. Control over relative humidity in the storage environment ameliorates the whole range of problems connected with the expansion and softening of gelatin caused by moisture.

COLLODION

The treatment of cellulose from cotton or wood with a mixture of nitric and sulfuric acids produces a substance known as pyroxylin, one of many forms of cellulose nitrate. Pyroxylin dissolved in alcohol and ether produces *collodion*, a transparent, viscous fluid. Discovered in 1847, collodion attracted interest because it formed transparent films when the solvents evaporated.

Pure collodion layers are not very flexible or permeable to water. When collodion was used in photography as a binder for prints, plasticizers, such as castor oil or glycerin, were added to give it flexibility and permeability.[33] Collodion layers often become brittle from loss of plasticizer or from an initial insufficiency of plasticizer. Brittleness and stresses lead to the formation of cracks in the collodion layer. These remain as hairline cracks but do not become large fissures as they do in albumen layers. Collodion swells somewhat in the presence of moisture, but much less than gelatin or albumen. Collodion layers are easily subject to abrasion. While its chemical deterioration is not well understood, collodion has none of albumen's tendency to yellow, nor does it exhibit the instability of thicker cellulose nitrate film bases. Collodion can be softened or dissolved by a large number of solvents.

PAPER SUPPORTS

The component of a photographic material on which the binder rests is known as the *support*. Binder layers are of necessity very thin. They do not have the mechanical strength or optical properties to be a complete photographic object. If no binder is present in a print material, the image resides in and among the upper fibers of the paper support.

Regardless of the nature of the final image material or the binder (if any), all 19th-century photographic prints have a support of high quality paper. When photography began in the 1840s, the raw materials for papermaking were cotton or flax (linen). The innate quality and purity of these fibers insured the durability of the paper made from them. While the basic fiber sources and sizing materials (usually alum-rosin) were the same for book and photographic papers, experience soon indicated that in order to withstand processing solutions, photographic paper had to be manufactured to previously unknown standards of purity and uniformity. A specialized industry arose to meet these production demands.

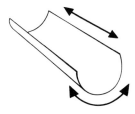

The curling of machine-made paper in response to changes in relative humidity occurs mostly in one direction. This is because the paper making machine caused most of the fibers to align themselves parallel to the moving web of paper.

Consequently, the paper supports of photographic prints, taken on their own, are among the most stable of all paper objects. Photographic paper supports were machine-made which provided a directional orientation to their physical properties. Paper is a moisture-absorbing substance which shrinks and becomes brittle in dry conditions, and expands and becomes flexible under moist conditions. When exposed to moisture, the cotton or linen fibers used as paper supports swell much more in width than in length. During the formation of the sheet on a paper machine, the fibers tend to align predominantly in one direction, that of the moving web of paper. This is called the "machine direction" or "grain direction"; the direction perpendicular to it is the "cross direction." When the finished sheet is exposed to moisture, the alignment of the fibers causes expansion mostly in the cross direction. The fiber alignment also causes differences in tensile strength and resistance to tearing when measured along the machine or cross directions.

All paper objects, even the high quality papers used in photography, are susceptible to photochemical damage and to deterioration from adverse environmental conditions. Light—especially from sources rich in ultraviolet radiation, such as direct sunlight, daylight, or fluorescent light—degrades and discolors paper. It is therefore necessary to regulate carefully the type, intensity, and duration of illumination when displaying photographic print materials in which light may reach the paper support. High relative humidity and elevated temperatures speed up the deterioration of paper and cause brittleness and discoloration. Mold and microbial growth are favored under moist conditions above 70% RH. Air pollution, including dust and soot, also poses a threat to paper.[34]

Some photographic print materials from the last two decades of the 19th century have a paper support with a superficial coating of barium sulfate in gelatin, known as a "baryta layer." Barium sulfate (also known as baryta or *blanc fixe*) is a white pigment which is very chemically stable. The baryta coating on photographic base paper was built up through three or four successive applications of a paste of gelatin/barium sulfate, with smoothing and texturizing operations carried out between coatings. The baryta layer poses few stability problems, and its opacity shields the paper fibers underneath it from light damage. The baryta layer is also a partial barrier to the diffusion of substances from poor quality mount boards which would stain the gelatin binder.

SECONDARY SUPPORTS

The paper support of many types of 19th-century prints—including, most notably, albumen prints—was not thick or sturdy enough to stay flat or resist damage in normal handling and use. When a binder layer is coated on one side of a paper support, any difference in the rate of expansion or contraction between the binder and support will cause curling or cockling of the print. Any cockling or plane deformation of the surface of prints with glossy binders will also cause specular reflections which make it difficult to view the prints. To solve the curl and specular reflection problem, and for aesthetic and protective reasons, many prints were adhered to rigid mounts. Any accessory material to which a print is adhered is known as a *secondary support*. Mount boards are the most common examples. In most cases (though the judgment is curatorial or aesthetic), a secondary support is regarded as part of the photograph.

Poor quality mount boards and a variety of structural problems which damage the primary support and binder layer are the most frequent difficulties related to the use of secondary supports. Mount boards are made by laminating layers of paper together. Their quality, like that of any paper object, depends mainly on the fiber source used. The earliest mount boards, those made before 1870, tended to be of good quality because techniques for making paper from inferior fiber sources, like wood pulp, had not yet been developed. Once low quality papers made partially or entirely from wood pulp became available, the overall quality of photographic mount boards declined.

The essential problem with using wood fiber sources for paper is the presence of *lignin*, a non-cellulose impurity which is very difficult to remove during paper-making. Lignin discolors and embrittles paper over time, especially in the presence of moisture or light. Newsprint deteriorates rapidly because of its high lignin content. The decomposition products of lignin also migrate to the binder layer of photographic prints, fading the image and causing yellow staining in albumen and gelatin. A common technique in manufacturing photographic mount boards was to use top and bottom sheets of thin, good quality paper with a core of thicker, highly lignified, poor quality paper.

The brittleness of deteriorated mounts also threatens photographs. All prints on embrittled mounts should be given a rigid secondary support of good quality board to supplement the original mount and to prevent damage in handling or storage. Care should be taken when storing prints so that mount boards are not left in contact with other photographs, as they would be in a stack of photographs without sleeves or interleaving.

Stresses created by adhering a print to a rigid secondary support cause another set of stability problems. In response to humidity

Lignin, a non-cellulose impurity in wood and paper products made from wood, can cause staining of albumen and gelatin. This albumen print has been heavily stained by contact with a poor-quality oval mat which contained lignin.

James M. Reilly

changes, gelatin and albumen binders expand and contract more than their paper supports, causing curl. When these movements are restrained by a rigid secondary support, stresses are created which can delaminate the print from the mount or tear the support and binder layer. Prints that have been adhered to mounts in only a few areas (usually at the corners) are especially vulnerable to this sort of damage.

SURFACE TREATMENTS AND ADHESIVES

The overall stability of photographic prints is also affected by substances applied as adhesives or surface treatments. Although surface coatings were not routinely applied to 19th-century prints, some exceptions are worth noting.

Surface coatings were applied to alter the surface character of prints, to protect them against atmospheric influences, and to serve as a preparative ground or consolidant for applied color. Many substances, including gelatin, waxes, and varnishes of various kinds, were applied to salted paper prints to give them a glossier print surface. The surface of an albumen print was already glossy, and mechanical smoothing in burnishing machines made it even glossier. However, mixtures of castile soap and turpentine were sometimes applied to prevent the albumen from sticking to the burnishing machine. "Lubricators," as they were known at the time, were not used when gelatin or collodion prints were burnished.

Some surface coatings were applied in the belief that they would provide protection against atmospheric influences. Substances such as varnish, gelatin, collodion, or wax actually did little good in protecting against atmospheric oxidants, moisture, or sulfiding gases. Even when a seal against the atmosphere was provided, as with varnish, moisture and pollutants can diffuse through the paper support and affect the image. Varnishes discolor, especially in light, and become embrittled.

Surface coatings also served as a ground or fixative for applied color. All of the materials and techniques available to artists during the 19th century were tried on photographs. Applied color ranged from a dab over lips and cheeks to complete overpainting in oils. Gum arabic or varnish was commonly used as a supercoat over applied watercolor on albumen prints. The albumen surface took watercolors well without any preparation, but after considerable color had been applied, it was felt that a unifying surface coat was necessary. Applied colors can be found on all types of photographs, with the exception of collodion prints.

Adhesives used during the 19th century to adhere prints to secondary supports included animal glues, gum arabic, gelatin, dextrin, and, most commonly, wheat starch paste. Prints were usually mounted while in a wet and expanded condition, and were dried under pressure or burnished before drying was complete. Poor quality adhesives, or those in which bacterial action is advanced, can stain or fade prints over time. Other indirect problems are caused by the hygroscopic nature of certain adhesives, notably proteins. The moisture absorbed by adhesives contributes to a faster rate of oxidation of image silver in areas directly above thick accretions of adhesives.

PRESERVATION PROBLEMS RELATED TO THE LAMINATE STRUCTURE OF PHOTOGRAPHIC PRINTS

Except for the usually binderless print materials—salted paper prints, platinotypes, and cyanotypes—the structure of a photographic print material is essentially that of a binder layer coated on a paper support. It is important to understand that the intimate bond between binder and support unites two dissimilar materials whose response to environmental conditions may be quite different.[35] Paper, gelatin, and albumen are all water-absorbing materials which expand as they absorb moisture and contract as moisture is lost. The problem is one of degree and rate. When one component expands or contracts faster than another, compressive or tensile stresses are generated which can fracture or rip the component. For example, albumen prints have a thin paper support and a binder which tends to contract and become brittle with age.

Quite curly even at normal humidity conditions, under moderately dry conditions unmounted albumen prints curl with the albumen on the inside into tight rolls as small as cigarettes. The curling runs parallel to the machine direction of the paper support because of the alignment of paper fibers along that axis. Tight curling usually causes a network of parallel cracks in the albumen layer along the same axis because the albu-

31

men is not flexible enough to withstand compressive stresses. A knowledge of the behavior of unmounted albumen prints allows one to anticipate and avoid curl problems. Fracturing need not occur if prints are housed in a sleeve or mat with a rigid secondary support. With the tight curl restrained by a protective enclosure and the curling tendency moderated by keeping relative humidity between 30 and 40%, unmounted albumen prints may be safely stored or handled.

The problems arising from the laminate structure of binder and support are compounded when a print is adhered to a rigid secondary support. The rigidity of mounts for prints varies, and most mounts become warped or bowed by prints, partially relieving the stresses. If a wetted and expanded print is adhered to a truly rigid support, the stresses which occur during drying and later in storage may be devastating to the binder lay-

er. Problems of this sort are seen when expanded albumen prints are dried under restraint on rigid materials, or when gelatin prints are "dry mounted" to rigid materials. Fissuring in the albumen print may become worse from such treatment, and a gelatin print drying under restraint may crack in response to humidity changes. Rigid secondary supports provide even more resistance to the side of the binder/support laminate that is already the least responsive to moisture. Moisture absorption may be uneven, causing localized stresses.

These are only a few examples of the structural problems associated with complex laminate structures of photographic prints. Such potential problems must be taken into consideration when establishing environmental conditions for storing a photographic collection, when designing protective packaging, and when devising conservation treatments.

Chapter III:

STABILITY OF SPECIFIC PRINT MATERIALS

The previous chapter presented a general discussion of the stability problems associated with the materials and structures of 19th-century photographic prints. This chapter addresses the specific stability problems and deterioration characteristics of the individual processes.

SALTED PAPER PRINTS

Salted paper prints have a simple, binderless print structure and respond to humidity changes in much the same way as any other fine quality, machine-made paper. The photolytic silver image on a salted paper print is formed in the topmost paper fibers, and it can be damaged when those fibers are abraded or when the paper is flexed enough to rupture them. Any form of color applied to the image is also very susceptible to abrasion. Many characteristic forms of paper deterioration may be present in salted paper prints, including foxing (described later), discoloration, stains, weaknesses, brittleness, thinned areas, and tears. Surface grime and dust are also common

problems, but attempts at cleaning are best left to a photographic conservator.

All of the deterioration forms characteristic of photolytic silver images are found in salted paper prints.[36] In its original state, the salted paper image is brown or reddish-brown in color; if gold-toned, it is purplish-brown. The symptoms of oxidative-reductive deterioration in salted paper prints are loss of highlight detail, overall fading, and a change in image hue toward redder or yellower shades. Because moisture and air are the primary causes of image deterioration, salted paper prints and many other types of silver prints tend to fade in a "picture frame" pattern from the outside edges in toward the center. Edge fading is caused by the simple fact that moisture and air have access to images from the edges when prints are piled in stacks or mounted in albums. The entire image can also deteriorate, with or without acute fading at the edges.

Photolytic silver images are characteristically unstable, and virtually all of them except those toned with a

These two salted paper prints (both from a calotype negative by Hill and Adamson) show typical symptoms of oxidative deterioration: edge fading, loss of highlight detail, and overall fading. Note the faded streaks and brush marks which resulted from the use of a hygroscopic mounting paste. The print at left has deteriorated much further than the one at right.

IMP/GEH

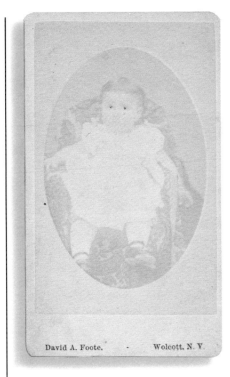

This albumen print has severely faded due to inadequate washing. The dark retouching spots in the eyes (which once blended invisibly) are a clue to how much of the original density has been lost.

James M. Reilly

David A. Foote. - Wolcott, N. Y.

any toning treatment. So much experimentation was done with salted paper print processing that it is difficult to make a positive identification of toning treatments or deterioration causes without resorting to elaborate analytical procedures.

Another common source of image deterioration in salted paper prints is metal flecks embedded in the paper support. These originated from the paper-making machinery or from brass buttons or other metal contaminants in the rags used to make the paper. The flecks usually appear on the image as a white spot with a dark, irregular speck in the center. Under magnification, the central speck appears as a dendritic (tree- or fern-like) shining piece of metal. The white area surrounding it is caused by the

combination of gold and platinum have significantly deteriorated. Salted paper prints frequently exhibit this instability, and the extent of their overall fading can often be estimated from retouched image areas. Watercolor or ink was originally applied to conceal defects and blend in with the silver image. These retouched areas now stand out on faded prints as anomalous dark spots and are sometimes mistaken for a form of deterioration. They provide a significant clue to the image's original intensity and image hue. The same phenomenon can also be found in other types of silver printing-out papers, especially albumen prints.

Sulfiding deterioration is common in salted paper prints because the principles of proper fixing and washing were not well understood during the 1840s and early 1850s, when most salted paper prints were made. In addition to unintentional sulfiding due to ignorance of processing methods, sulfiding was widely used as a toning treatment. In the intermediate stages of sulfiding, salted paper prints have blacker than usual image hues and often fade to yellow in the lighter image tones. More advanced sulfiding leaves salted paper prints completely faded, with a greenish-yellow image hue and often with stained non-image areas. Most salted paper prints which survive in good condition were either toned with gold or prepared without

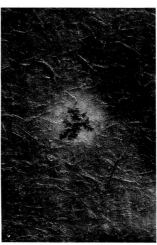

Metal flecks embedded in the paper support cause a faded spot to appear in salted paper or albumen prints. Such a spot is evident on the right knee of the child in this albumen print. At 30X magnification, (bottom), a tree-like, shining speck of metal can be observed in the center of the faded area.

James M. Reilly
Photomacrograph,
Caterina Salvi

metal's desensitizing effect, which prevented an image from forming there during the exposure of the print. Silver ions are powerful oxidants and will replace metals that are lower in the electrochemical series. Any copper or iron in the metal fleck was therefore replaced by silver and became oxidized to iron or copper ions. When the print was exposed, the silver ions had already replaced the iron or copper and were not available to form a photographic image in the area surrounding the fleck. Embedded metal impurities became less common once paper began to be manufactured expressly for photographic use.

ALBUMEN PRINTS

STRUCTURAL PROBLEMS AND DETERIORATION OF THE ALBUMEN LAYER

The major forms of deterioration in albumen prints are changes in the photolytic silver image, embrittle-

made before 1870 were less heavily coated than those made later and have therefore survived better. All albumen prints, however, have suffered to some extent from a gradual yellowing of the albumen layer. The potential for yellowing from one chemical mechanism, the Maillard or "protein-sugar" reaction, was lessened if, prior to coating, the albumen was subjected to a process of bacterial fermentation.[31] Most industrial producers of albumen paper used the fermentation process. But yellowing has many causes, and nearly all albumen prints have moderate to severe yellowing in non-image areas. The extent of yellowing is chiefly regulated by the relative humidity of the storage environment and by the amount of photochemical damage done to the print while on display.

Archivists and paper conservators are familiar with *foxing*, a type of paper staining characterized by blotchy, reddish-brown patches. Foxing can be seen on some albumen prints and is often confined to either

Many of the most commonly observed forms of deterioration are apparent in this albumen print. These include highlight yellowing, overall fading, a shift in image hue towards yellowish-brown, loss of highlight detail, and the brown spots known as foxing.

James M. Reilly

ment, staining and yellowing of the albumen layer, and structural problems leading to severe cracking and fissuring of the albumen layer. Problems directly related to the physical and chemical properties of albumen occur in proportion to the thickness of the albumen layer. Albumen prints

the mount or the print, but can sometimes be found on both. The causes of foxing are still not well understood. It is usually associated with iron or copper impurities in paper but can also be caused by mold growth. These causes have been known to operate both simultaneously and independently.[37] Often the brown spots will fluoresce when illuminated with an ultraviolet source. Under microscopic examination, some foxed areas on albumen prints are seen to surround embedded metal particles. In other cases, no metal fragments or remains of fungal growth are visible. In any event, the occurrence of foxing is linked to the relative humidity of the storage environment and is much more prevalent under high RH conditions.

The brittleness which characterizes deteriorated or excessively dry albumen layers makes them vulnerable to damage with rough handling. Unmounted prints are likely to crease when picked up with one hand, and the albumen often fractures in a semicircular pattern. Folding mounted or unmounted prints fractures the albumen layer, and may rupture paper fibers and detach pieces of albumen along the crease.

Cracking and fissuring are another serious form of deterioration in albumen layers. Albumen made brittle by dryness or deteriorative chemical changes may crack from the restraint imposed by a rigid mount, the compressive stresses of unrestrained inward curling, or direct impact shocks to the surface. Tight inward curling usually results in a series of parallel cracks in the machine direction of the support. Cracks emerge as small fractures in the albumen layer but eventually widen to expose the underlying paper fibers. The cracks in many prints have a random, intersecting pattern, and the widening fissures and upward cupping of the albumen fragments gradually turn the albumen layer into a "mud-flat" of isolated concave flakes.[35] The risk of losing individual pieces of albumen increases as the albumen layer disintegrates. Severely cracked, cupped surfaces attract dirt and trap it beneath and between the albumen flakes. Surface cleaning is quite obviously difficult under these circumstances.

Cracking and fissuring are best observed under a microscope, but in advanced stages can be detected by the eye alone. Wetting and drying cracked albumen layers, especially when they are on a print that is mounted or must otherwise dry under restraint, will worsen the cracking. This must be borne in mind when considering whether to unmount a print. There are, at present, no entirely safe and satisfactory methods for remounting an albumen print, and large prints are too prone to curling to be matted without remounting.

Surface abrasion poses a threat to thicker and smoother albumen layers. Heavily burnished albumen prints are particularly susceptible to

Unrestrained curling of an albumen print (left) has resulted in the formation of a series of parallel cracks. Though difficult to see with the naked eye, the cracks are readily visible at 30X magnification (upper right).

James M. Reilly
Photomacrograph,
Caterina Salvi

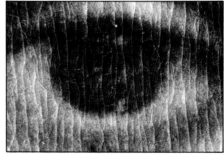

Another form of cracking found in albumen prints has a random, intersecting pattern of cracks and fissures in the albumen layer (30X magnification).

Photomacrograph,
Caterina Salvi

abrasion. Mounted albumen prints usually have a concave shape due to the inward pull of the albumen layers and abrasion is often found along the raised side or on the center of the print where another concave print rested. Many 19th-century album designs, especially those in the cabinet-card format, actually force prints on facing pages to abrade each other. Abrasion can cause the loss of pieces of the albumen layer in prints with advanced cracking and general deterioration.

Another form of deterioration connected with storage materials is the staining of the albumen layer from contact with poor quality papers and cardboard that contain groundwood. This effect is often seen as a "window" of brownish stains on a print in the shape of the opening cut in an album page or, in the case of a framed

print, a mat. The stain forms wherever the highly lignified paper touches the print, while the area of the opening remains relatively unstained. The opposite effect, in which prints yellow where not protected by an overmat, is caused by photochemical damage from prolonged display.

FADING OF ALBUMEN TINTING DYES

Tinting dyes were colorants added to albumen prior to coating. Their purpose was to give an overall color cast to the highlight areas of the image and to mask the yellowing of the albumen. Tinting dyes should be distinguished from colorants applied to finished prints to redden cheeks, color clothing, and otherwise decorate local areas of the image.

The pink, blue, and purple synthetic dyes used to tint albumen layers

The effects of prolonged display and poor quality framing and matting materials are illustrated in this albumen print. Areas of the image which were covered by the lignin-containing overmat have become stained, particularly at the mat's edge.

James M. Reilly

are extremely unstable, especially to light.[30] Their color, like that of other dyes, is lost or modified during chemical reactions. Dye fading may occur either as a result of exposure to light, or in the dark under conditions of elevated temperature and humidity. Although many albumen prints made between 1870 and 1900 are on tinted paper, the dyes have usually faded and their presence is difficult to detect.

Hand-coloring in the form of watercolor or dyes can be destroyed by extended display. This late 19th-century albumen print was once extensively hand-colored. Only the areas protected by an overmat, such as the green-colored area at the top, have survived.

James M. Reilly

A characteristic form of deterioration of albumen tinting dyes is localized fading caused when part of a print was protected from light exposure or shielded from atmospheric influences. This fading most often forms a border where the edges of the print were protected by an overmat during display. Highlight areas under the mat will still be pink or purple, while only yellowed albumen is visible in the areas exposed to light. The same effects can be seen in prints from albums. Most album pages cover a portion of the print, and in many cases the portion protected by the album page has noticeably more tinting dye than the rest of the print. Poor quality album pages can cause the opposite effect: the part of the print in contact with the album page will have the most dye fading. Even a very brief exposure to light will significantly fade tinting dyes, and great care should be exercised in displaying tinted prints.

Dye fading which occurs in the dark under adverse temperature and humidity conditions is usually uniform

and accompanied by silver image fading and albumen yellowing. With some practice and experience, it is possible to visually identify tinted albumen prints which have lost all of their original tint. Pink dyes that have completely faded sometimes leave a subtle "buff" or "chamois" color cast in highlight areas. Prints which initially had the most dye tend to have the most obvious clues to the presence of faded dye.

IMAGE DETERIORATION IN ALBUMEN PRINTS

In their original condition, albumen prints have non-image areas that are white or slightly tinted with pink or blue dyes. Their images are brown, purple, or nearly blue-black. The delicate tonality and lovely image quality of undeteriorated prints sur-

vive in few examples; between 90 and 95% of all albumen prints have faded and changed color. Albumen prints share the unstable photolytic image structure of salted paper prints and have generally similar deterioration patterns. Fading is so prevalent in albumen and other types of printed-out

The characteristics of an albumen print in good condition are shown in this example: a purple-brown image color, a full tonal scale, white highlights, and excellent highlight detail.

James M. Reilly

38

silver prints that some noticeable deterioration is almost always present, either in localized areas or overall. Any print that closely resembles albumen but is absolutely pristine and unfaded is probably not an albumen print at all, but a photomechanical print (collotype or woodburytype) or a carbon print. Indeed, although fading and yellowing are widely identified with albumen prints, few people appreciate how much image loss most prints have suffered.

Image fading in albumen prints is primarily a function of exposure to moisture and occurs mainly through an oxidation-reduction mechanism.[15] Its manifestations are loss of highlight detail, overall fading of the image, and a change in image color from purplish-brown to a warmer, yellower brown. Detail in faces and clothing, or in any light area of the image, tends to disappear. These manifestations are characteristic of oxidative-reductive deterioration in all gold-toned photolytic silver images.

Oxidative-Reductive Deterioration

Photolytic (printed-out) silver images of all types make up about 90% of 19th-century photographic prints. They fade in inverse proportion to their original density; in other words, the more density an image started with, the more resistant it is to fading. This fact is frequently expressed in 19th-century literature about preserving photographs, and it has a physical basis in the way the oxidative-reductive deterioration process works.

Oxidative-reductive deterioration is a cycle of chemical changes involving the oxidation of image silver to colorless silver ions and the reduction of these silver ions back to the metallic state at another location in the image layer. In high-density areas where many silver particles are in close proximity, the silver ions formed during oxidation tend to reduce onto nearby particles. Although the image particles undergo a progressive re-formation, at any given moment most of the silver is in the metallic state and much of the density is retained. In low- and middle-density areas, there are smaller and fewer particles, giving the silver ions formed through oxidation less chance to be reduced back to metallic silver. This is because fewer silver ions are formed in these areas (a high silver ion concentration favors reduction) and there are fewer particles nearby to serve as reduction sites, making the silver ions more likely to remain in the colorless ionic form.

The steady migration of silver ions away from the main image area and into other parts of the print gradually drains the supply of silver for the reformation of the image, and more and more density is lost. As a result, the lighter tones disappear first, the middle tones next, and the shadows last.

The penetration of moisture into albums, books, and stacks of photographs may be uneven and often starts from the edges and goes in toward the center of the print. Uneven access of air and moisture creates endless variations of localized fading. Hygroscopic mounting pastes can cause fading in the shape of brush marks. In some albums, photographs mounted on facing pages contact each other when the album is closed. These prints are typically less faded in the areas of contact because the contact forms a barrier to air and moisture. Overall fading usually occurs together with localized fading because the conditions for localized attack or protection do not normally exist for the whole life of the print. We owe the existence of the few albumen prints left in pristine condition to their having been protected from atmospheric influences by being stored in a naturally dry climate or in tightly closed trunks, boxes, and albums under dry conditions.

The fate of the majority of albumen prints conclusively proves that display, frequent use, and exposure to the ordinary environmental conditions of temperate climates will cause serious image deterioration within a fairly short time—certainly within 30 to 50 years. We have only a few chances left to prevent these deteriorative processes from attacking the handful of prints fortunate enough to have survived in a protected environment.

Image Fading Caused By Bronze Powder

A particular type of localized fading in albumen prints can be caused by some of the gilt inks used to decorate album pages and mounting boards.[38] Nearly all *cartes des visite* made during the 1860s had two thin gilt lines imprinted as a decorative border on the mounting card. When the larger, cabinet-size format later became popular, dark brown or purple mounts were common. These were often imprinted with the photographer's name in gilt ink. The gilding of mount edges was also common during the 1870s, 1880s, and early 1890s; and gilt inks were liberally used to decorate album pages.

The gilt inks used were usually not gold but "bronze powder," an alloy of copper and zinc that sometimes included tin. Zinc has such dire effects on photographs that zinc dust has been applied to prints as an accelerated image-stability test. It is therefore not surprising that there are many examples of localized fading caused by gilt inks. This fading has two characteristic forms: isolated faded spots caused by small individual flakes of metallic ink pigment, and faded patterns in the shape of the gilt ink design when a print has been pasted on top of the ink. The flaking of the metallic pigments and subsequent fading when the particles come to rest in the image areas of the print is the most common form of the problem. The yellowed, faded spots occasionally have a shiny, mirrored surface. In addition, when a white area of a print covers a gilt ink design on a mount, a yellow-green stain in the shape of the design appears.

The deterioration problems associated with gilt inks are likely to continue as long as prints are not properly handled and stored in individual protective enclosures. As with all other oxidative forms of silver image deterioration, the severity of the problem will depend to a large extent on the ambient relative humidity of the storage environment.

Gilt inks used on mount boards for decorative purposes sometimes caused fading. In this example, small faded spots can be seen in all areas of the albumen print image (left). An enlarged detail of the border area (top right) shows how the metallic gilt ink particles have flaked off and become distributed over the print surface. When the ink particles settled in an image area (bottom right), they oxidized the silver image, resulting in a faded spot (both at 30X magnification).

James M. Reilly
Photomacrographs,
Caterina Salvi

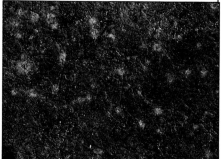

40

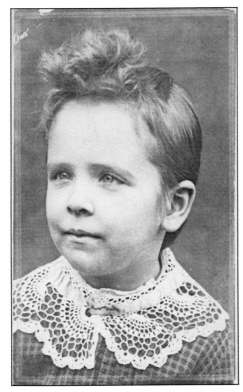

Other forms of damage occurred when photographs were mounted on top of gilt inks containing bronze powder. When the gilt lines were covered by the photographic image, uniform fading resulted (top). Areas without a photographic image usually became stained with a greenish discoloration wherever they covered gilt inks (bottom). Photomacrographs of the affected areas (30X magnification) accompany each example.

James M. Reilly
Photomacrographs,
Caterina Salvi

Sulfiding Deterioration

Sulfiding deterioration in albumen prints has two forms: one caused by thiosulfate retained after insufficient washing or from atmospheric sulfiding gases, and the other caused by silver thiosulfate retained due to the use of exhausted fixing solutions.[20] When sulfiding takes place without extra silver present, the image fades to a yellow-brown or slightly greenish color, and the highlights have an unusually strong yellow-brown stain. When silver thiosulfates are present, the image fades to a greenish-black color with more highlight detail; there is much more staining, usually greenish-yellow, of non-image areas. With experience, it is fairly easy to identify albumen prints which show effects of bad processing from those which show effects of the more typical oxidative-reductive fading.

Deterioration from poor original processing is more common in mass-produced albumen prints, especially in low-cost or pirated copy editions, than in careful amateur work or studio portraits. As a group, low-cost stereo views seem to display sulfiding deterioration more than any other type of albumen print. But no more than about 15% of all deteriorated prints can be clearly identified as having sulfided due to poor processing.

Sulfiding deterioration from both inadequate washing and an exhausted fixing solution have caused fading and staining in this albumen print.

James M. Reilly

PROBLEMS CAUSED BY IMPROPER DISPLAY

Albumen prints displayed for prolonged periods have characteristic deterioration problems. Their albumen layer is usually quite heavily yellowed from photochemical damage. This staining can be made worse by lignin decomposition products from mount boards or overmats with a high groundwood content. A frame's thin wooden backing board can also stain a photograph. Substances from the board migrate onto the print mount and cause "woodburn," in which the grain pattern, knots, gaps, and other surface features of the board show as a stain pattern on the bottom of the mount. In severe cases, the products released from the backing board eventually migrate through the mount and stain the photograph. This is especially true for albumen prints because their primary support is so thin and because they have no baryta layer to block the diffusion of lignin decomposition products. Prints displayed for long periods usually have faded images; their shadow areas in many cases have a shiny, bluish-silver mirror. If any part of the print mount was left exposed to light, it too will be stained. Typically, the outlines of an overmat are clearly visible as a less discolored area.

PLATINOTYPES

The principal forms of deterioration in platinotypes affect the primary or

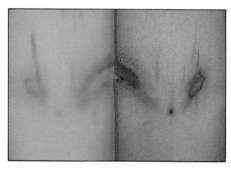

secondary support but not the metallic platinum image. Very little if any change occurs in the platinotype image under even the most adverse environmental circumstances.[39] However, as if to offset its remarkable image stability, the platinotype has far more stability problems with its paper support than other binderless print materials do.

Platinotypes commonly have yellowed and embrittled paper supports as a result of several factors, including the nature of the chemicals used in processing, the quality of the paper support itself, the properties of the platinum image, and the absence of a binder layer. The sensitizing solutions for the platinotype include iron compounds, which can contribute to the deterioration of the paper support if not completely removed during processing. An acid rinse to help remove these iron compounds was the final step in processing, but could itself weaken the paper support. The catalytic activity of the metallic platinum image can contribute to discoloration and embrittlement of the support-port. The absence of a binder exposes the cellulose of the support to more photochemical damage during display. Because of the probable weakened condition of the paper support of platinotypes, light levels during display should be carefully monitored, and yellowed or embrittled prints should not be displayed at all. The general weakness of their support makes it especially important to provide a rigid secondary support for platinotypes during storage and handling. The high catalytic activity of the platinum image also makes it necessary to provide protective packaging to keep platinotypes from affecting other objects stored with them.

CYANOTYPES

Cyanotypes do not have a binder layer and so avoid binder-related deterioration problems. In general, cyanotypes have deteriorated much less than the various silver print materials used during the 19th century. The principal forms of deterioration in cyanotypes are staining, discoloration and embrittlement of the paper support, and fading of the blue image.

The paper supports of cyanotypes have fewer stability problems than those of platinotypes, even though both processes utilize iron compounds, which are associated with several forms of paper deterioration. The acid rinse during processing and the catalytic activity of the platinum image may contribute to the faster rate of paper deterioration in platinotypes. Cyanotypes still occasionally display overall discoloration, local brown stains, foxing and embrittlement; and, like any paper object, they may discolor from contact with poor quality mounting boards or adhesives.

The blue images of cyanotypes are usually in good condition, though some prints have faded. While they are known to fade in light and to revive partially when stored in the dark, in general, the behavior of cyanotype images is not well understood. Faded examples may have evidence of light damage (for example, a dark border where the image was protected from light by an overmat) or may be faded overall. Because the image will fade under alkaline conditions, alkaline-buffered enclosures should not be used with cyanotypes.

Cyanotypes have no binder of gelatin or albumen to absorb some of the wavelengths of light which are most harmful to cellulose, and thus partially protect the support. Since both the image and support are vulnerable to photochemical damage, display times and illumination levels for cyanotypes should be carefully regulated. Cyanotypes are easily torn because they lack the mechanical strength provided by a binder.

CARBON PRINTS, WOODBURYTYPES, AND GUM BICHROMATE PRINTS

Because they use pigments as the final image material, carbon prints, woodburytypes, and gum bichromate prints have excellent image stability; very little or no fading can be observed in them. The major forms of deterioration in carbon prints and woodburytypes are associated with the gelatin binder. The most common problem is the cracking of the gelatin in the darkest areas of the print, where the binder layer is thickest. This problem is most acute with woodburytypes, but sometimes occurs in carbon prints. The cracks are large and very apparent upon visual inspection. Another binder-related problem with carbon prints and woodburytypes is a strong tendency to curl when not mounted to a rigid secondary support. In gum bichromate prints, the gum arabic binder is seldom deposited thickly enough to manifest cracking.

COLLODION PRINTING-OUT PAPERS

Deterioration in collodion printing-out papers occurs principally as a result of structural problems, abrasion of the collodion layer, or changes in the photolytic silver image. The laminate structure of collodion prints consists of a paper support, a baryta layer, and a collodion layer. Collodion prints were manufactured with matte and glossy surfaces. The glossy variety have a thicker baryta layer with a very smooth continuous surface and a thick collodion layer. Matte collodion prints have a thinner baryta layer, with a surface texture which follows the contours of the paper support, and a collodion layer that is also quite thin. Collodion layers do not absorb moisture and swell as the paper support and baryta layer do, so stresses can be generated when changes in humidity make the support expand or contract. Such tensile or compressive stresses are damaging because the collodion layer is not very flexible. Many hairline cracks and fractures due to blows and flexing can be observed in collodion prints, especially those with glossy surfaces. Because of its brittleness, rigid secondary supports should always be provided to prevent collodion from flexing during handling.

Abrasion is a serious problem with collodion prints because of their poor resistance to abrasion and the extreme thinness of the collodion layer. Characteristic forms of abrasion damage include scratches, gouges, and roughened, dull spots. Disfiguring white spots are created whenever the collodion containing the image is abraded enough to expose the underlying baryta layer. Some types of glossy collodion paper manufactured in the early 1890s had even thinner and more delicate collodion layers than most.

Image deterioration in these papers is often accompanied by silver mirroring and abrasion damage. A distinctive "thinness" in the appearance of the collodion layer can also usually be seen. Matte collodion prints are also prone to abrasion damage, although it disfigures them less than it does glossy prints. Textured paper stocks—those embossed with the patterns of linen cloth, small pyramids, and other textures—were occasionally used as the support for matte collodion prints. These prints seem particularly susceptible to abrasion damage. Because of the nature of collodion itself, the yellowing of collodion layers due to their chemical instability or contact with lignified papers and boards is not as serious a problem as it is with albumen prints.[40] However, local brown stains may be present on collodion prints from mold growth or severe foxing on the mount.

Image deterioration in collodion prints follows the same general course as in albumen prints and gelatin printing-out papers. On glossy collodion papers where only gold toning was used, the typical appearances of oxidative-reductive deterioration include loss of highlight detail,

a shift in image color from purple to a warm reddish-brown, and overall fading. Matte collodion prints typically have much better image stability. The processing of these prints included a combination of gold and platinum toning which not only changed the image color to a neutral or sometimes greenish-black, but significantly improved the resistance of the image to oxidative attack. Some highlight detail loss and some fading may be present, but matte collodion prints usually stand out as being much less faded or mirrored than their gelatin, albumen, or glossy collodion counterparts.

Sulfiding deterioration in glossy collodion printing-out papers also resembles that in other photolytic silver images: a fading of the highlights and an intermediate stage of blackening of the image hue in the middletones and shadows, followed by complete fading of the image to a yellowish- or greenish-brown. Greenish-yellow stains will be present in non-image areas if an exhausted fixing solution was used during the original processing. Fading in matte collodion papers caused by thiosulfate retained after inadequate washing will generally be less severe because the silver, gold, and platinum image has a higher resistance to all forms of attack. Retained silver thiosulfates from exhausted fixing solutions will still cause greenish-yellow stains in non-image areas.

GELATIN PRINTING-OUT PAPERS

STRUCTURAL PROBLEMS OF GELATIN PRINTING-OUT PAPERS

Gelatin printing-out papers were mostly made with glossy surfaces, and had a laminate structure that included a paper support, a baryta layer, and a gelatin layer. The structural problems common to all barytapaper/ gelatin prints can be found in these prints, together with the typical stability problems of gold-toned, photolytic silver images. Combined gold and platinum toning was almost never applied to gelatin printing-out papers.

Three types of surface finishing treatments were used with gelatin printing-out papers: matte drying, ferrotyping, and burnishing. The surface of air-dried gelatin is quite matte in comparison with a highly burnished surface, but *ferrotyping*—in which a wet print was dried in contact with a highly polished surface of metal or glass—produced the smoothest surfaces of all. Ferrotyped surfaces often show the imprint of any dirt or imperfection on the metal or glass used to obtain the high gloss. Ferrotyped prints seem to be more brittle and subject to cracking than air-dried surfaces. Most studio portraits on gelatin printing-out paper were burnished rather than ferrotyped, because ferrotyping could not be done on mounted prints.

Unmounted gelatin printing-out papers are subject to the same curl problems which afflict all prints with gelatin binders.[38] The expansion and contraction of the gelatin binder due to changes in relative humidity are much greater than those of the paper support. Depending on the thickness of the support, curling occurs inward toward the gelatin under dry circumstances and outward toward the support when the gelatin expands under humid conditions. Dimensional changes in gelatin prints due to changing moisture content cause numerous plane deformations if prints are mounted with only a few "spots" of adhesive rather than with a relatively uniform coat. This restraint sets up localized stresses which lead to puckering or even tearing of the print in the area of adhesion. Such deterioration is typical of amateur albums, in which prints are often glued or "tipped" in—and broken off—at the corners.

Under moist conditions, gelatin absorbs water and becomes sticky and soft, making ferrotyping possible. If high humidity conditions prevail during extended storage, the surface character of prints can be modified by contact with smooth plastic enclosures; the gelatin binder may even adhere to the enclosure. Smooth, moisture-trapping plastic enclosure materials are therefore not recommended for collections subject to seasonal high humidities. Paper enclosures may also adhere to swelled gelatin in high RH, so climate control is the only real insurance against such damage.

Abrasion damage to the surface of gelatin printing-out papers is a common form of deterioration. The problem is most serious with mounted and burnished prints, on which any roughening of the surface causes a loss in the density of shadow areas. Deep scratches and abrasions expose the white baryta underneath. Abrasion can cause a localized "burnishing" or smoothing of the surface of matte gelatin papers, and this too is disfiguring.

IMAGE DETERIORATION IN GELATIN PRINTING-OUT PAPERS

Image deterioration in gelatin printing-out papers follows the general pattern of all gold-toned, photolytic silver images. The image is initially purple or purplish-brown, but fades in the presence of moisture and oxidants to a much redder and yellower brown. Highlight detail is lost, and the image becomes much lighter overall. Silver mirroring may appear in dark image areas.

Sulfiding deterioration is more common in gelatin printing-out papers than in albumen prints because the thicker support and baryta layer of the gelatin materials tend to retain more thiosulfate. With no baryta layer and a much thinner support, albumen prints require less washing to remove the thiosulfate fixing solution during processing. The appearance of sulfiding in gelatin printing-out papers is quite distinctive. Poor washing will leave behind considerable amounts of thiosulfate and cause rapid overall fading of the image to a yellowish- or greenish-brown image color, although non-image areas will remain mostly unaffected. If exhausted fixer was used during processing, a stain will show in non-image areas, and the image will retain more highlight detail. Silver mirroring may be present in either case, since some oxidative-reductive deterioration usually accompanies sulfiding. If less thiosulfate was retained, or if the print has been kept under very dry conditions, the sulfiding may be in an intermediate stage in which the image has not completely faded.

Gelatin printing-out papers display a characteristic set of symptoms during this partial conversion of the image silver to silver sulfide. The most prominent of these are a simultaneous loss of highlight detail and a "cooling" of the image color to a blacker

shade. At this point, the image has yellowed lighter tones, while middletone and shadow areas seem more neutral than is usual with this type of print. Because the decomposition of thiosulfate to active sulfur compounds is regulated by the amount of moisture available, these changes often follow the pattern of moisture absorption from the edges of a print in toward the center. The deeper tones become more neutral black in color and tend to fade to yellow more slowly than the middletones because there is more image silver in these areas. The complete conversion to yellowbrown silver sulfide (instead of the more neutral black silver/silver-sulfide combination) takes longer.

Sulfiding deterioration due to exhausted fixing solutions is less common than that caused by insufficient washing during processing. Obviously, any combination of relative amounts of pure thiosulfates from insufficient washing and silver thiosulfates from exhausted fixing baths is possible causing varying degrees of blackening, staining, and fading. In some cases, a partially sulfided gelatin printing-out paper can closely resemble a neutral black developedout print.

GELATIN DEVELOPING-OUT PAPERS

The various types of gelatin developing-out papers made during the last fifteen years of the 19th century include fast-speed silver bromide papers and the so-called "gaslight" or contact-speed silver chloride and chlorobromide papers. All have the same laminate structure of a support, a baryta layer, and a gelatin emulsion layer; and all share the set of prob-

lems deriving from the physical properties of gelatin. The curling problems, plane deformations, defective mounting techniques, and surface characteristics described in the section of this chapter dealing with gelatin printing-out papers are also typical of gelatin developing-out papers. The chemical composition of the image (silver and gold in the printing-out papers, and silver alone in the developing-out materials) and its relative particle size do not affect the physical properties and response to humidity changes of the binder and support components.

Gelatin developing-out papers were made in glossy and matte varieties, with various surface textures and weights of paper support. Tinting the baryta layer with pink or purple dyes was common with printing-out papers but not with developing-out papers because it did not harmonize well with their neutral black image color. Although gelatin developingout papers made before 1900 were occasionally ferrotyped to produce an ultra-glossy finish, most were airdried.

IMAGE DETERIORATION IN GELATIN DEVELOPING-OUT PAPERS

Image deterioration in gelatin developing-out papers follows a different course than in printing-out papers because of the structural differences between filamentary and photolytic silver. The most common types of image deterioration are caused by sulfiding due to improper processing and by an oxidative-reductive process. Symptoms of oxidative deterioration include overall fading, some loss of highlight detail, a yellowing of the lighter areas of the image and, very often, silver mirroring in shadow areas. In advanced cases of oxidative-reductive deterioration, the original black image color gives way to a faded yellow-brown with yellow highlights. These color changes are caused by physical changes in the tiny filaments of silver which make up the image on a submicroscopic level. During oxidative-reductive deterioration, the filaments are broken up into smaller particles which appear yellow.[21] The higher the initial density, the longer it takes for oxidative attack to break down the filament bundles into smaller pieces. Shadow areas get lighter and progress through warm black, brown, and yellowish-brown hues before completely fading to yellow. Non-image areas do not become heavily stained.

SILVER MIRRORING

Shiny, bluish silver mirroring is so characteristic of gelatin developing-out prints and all other kinds of filamentary-silver-in-gelatin images that it is a useful clue in identifying them. Nearly all 19th-century gelatin developing-out paper prints have some mirroring as a consequence of oxidative-reductive deterioration. In this process, silver ions migrate to the extreme uppermost surface of the gelatin layer and are then reduced back to the metallic state to form an almost continuous layer of small, tightly packed particles. (Ordinary glass mirrors are made by the controlled reduction of silver ions onto a glass surface.) The conditions which cause mirroring in some faded silver prints and not others are not completely understood.

Because mirroring is affected both by the amount of oxidation of the silver image and the conditions affecting reduction at the print surface, many non-uniformities and patterns are observable in mirrored prints. To properly observe mirroring, the print should be viewed from a low angle and tilted to create a direct specular reflection. Mirroring typically progresses from the outside edges of a print toward the center, following the path by which air and moisture gain access to the silver image and slowly oxidize it. If a print is only partially protected from air and moisture (for example, by a smaller object placed on it during long-term storage), the mirroring will occur every-

where but under the object, and it will trace the object's outline in a bluish sheen. Mold or surface abrasion will cause a local discontinuity in mirroring. Mirroring often occurs directly over areas where a hygroscopic mounting adhesive was used. Mirroring should not be removed from gelatin prints by abrasion or chemical treatment. Special care should be taken not to touch the surface of mirrored prints, because finger oils will cause changes in the surface.

SULFIDING DETERIORATION IN GELATIN DEVELOPING-OUT PAPERS

Sulfiding deterioration in gelatin developing-out papers has the same root causes as in other types of silver prints: insufficient washing, the use of exhausted fixing baths, and, to a lesser extent, the presence of atmospheric sulfiding gases. Its symptoms, however, more closely resemble oxidative-reductive deterioration and are not as distinctive as those in printing-out papers where sulfiding is characterized by an intermediate blackening of the image hue and an ultimate yellow-green color. Developed-out images are neutral black to begin with, so the partial sulfiding of the image silver does not cause any change in hue. When sulfiding is caused by retained thiosulfate from inadequate washing, the non-image areas remain white because there is no silver to react with sulfur and form yellow silver sulfide. The highlight areas of the image are converted first, then the middletones, and finally the shadows fade to a yellow (or in some cases yellowish-green) silver sulfide.

When silver thiosulfates from overused fixing baths are present, their stains form in non-image areas.[41] Mirroring may also be present, because neither oxidative-reductive deterioration nor sulfiding occurs often without some trace of the other. Local spots of sulfiding deterioration are common in all types of silver prints. They may be caused by thiosulfate spilled on the print, by a print having been grasped with hypo-laden hands during processing, or (perhaps most frequently) by the stacking of prints in the wash water. In the latter case, fading occurs in rectangular shapes or other sharp outlines that show where the print was partially covered during washing.

Chapter IV:

IDENTIFICATION OF 19TH-CENTURY PHOTOGRAPHIC AND PHOTOMECHANICAL PRINT PROCESSES

The identification of processes (i.e., the determination of the techniques and materials used in producing photographs) plays a crucial role in preservation. It is the basis for establishing the correct environmental conditions, handling practices, and storage enclosures for each type of photograph found in a collection. Among the diverse kinds of photographic artifacts, print processes are the most difficult to identify. The reasons for this are the large number of known processes and the fact that they often resemble each other quite closely. The last two decades of the 19th century comprise a period when both older and more modern materials coexisted, and prints of this vintage can be particularly challenging to identify.

The problem is also complicated by the emergence during the same period of photomechanical reproduction processes, in which photographic images could be reproduced on a printing press using inks or pigments. It is important to be able to distinguish a *true photographic print*—a piece of paper which at one time had been sensitive to light—from a *photomechanical print*. The latter type of print may bear a photographic image, but its key characteristic is that it was never itself light-sensitive. Rather, its image was impressed or transferred to the paper in some mechanical fashion, hence the term photomechanical print. Some photomechanical prints can be remarkably similar in appearance to true photographic prints, such as albumen prints or platinotypes.

This chapter addresses the problem of identifying 19th-century photographic prints by first presenting a general discussion of the necessary tools and preparation for the task. Next, in recognition of the fact that not all 19th-century positive images are paper prints, a brief discussion of how to identify daguerreotypes, ambrotypes, and tintypes is presented. The rest of the chapter consists of the *IDENTIFICATION GUIDE*, a systematic method for identifying the major types of 19th-century photographic and photomechanical prints. The *IDENTIFICATION GUIDE* has three parts: an organizational flowchart (pages 54–55), a textual description of what to look for and how to use the flowchart (pages 52–68), and thirdly, an alphabetical summary of physical descriptions for all the processes (pages 69–72). The information in this latter section is intended as a cross-check to verify the identity of a print process once a determination has been made using the flowchart.

The vast majority of 19th-century photographic prints were made on one of the silver printing-out papers described in Chapter I: salted paper, albumen paper, or gelatin or collodion printing-out paper. The ability to recognize each of these in their many forms is a valuable preservation skill. A great number of obscure processes and idiosyncratic variations of the major processes are mentioned in 19th-century photographic literature. Their prominence in manuals, especially early ones, is often out of proportion to their actual use. In first learning to identify photographic print processes, it is best to concentrate on the major materials and temporarily avoid the others.

Process identification is complicated not only by the variety of processes, but by individual variations in print finishing and presentation, and especially by the many possible forms of deterioration. The information given in the preceding chapters on print materials and components and their characteristic forms of deterioration is a necessary prerequisite for accurately identifying processes and dating photographs. It is frequently the case that deterioration (or the lack of it) provides a decisive clue in identifying a print process.

It should be noted that the ability to identify processes grows with practice and experience and cannot be entirely learned from this or any other book. Illustrations cannot fully convey the color, surface character, or any number of other distinguishing features of actual photographic objects. Anyone learning to accurately identify 19th-century photographic processes needs direct and extensive experience with photographs. Studying labeled examples is perhaps the most effective means of becoming familiar with the various processes.

PREPARATION AND TOOLS

The suggestions given in Chapter VII on print handling should be observed in examining photographs for identification purposes: have plenty of work space, make sure your hands are clean, proceed slowly, and take notes in pencil.

The most effective tool in process identification is the naked eye. To function properly, the eye needs enough light to accurately discern colors and fine textures. The perception of print color is affected by the nature of the light source illuminating it. The purple-brown color of albumen prints, for example, looks somewhat different under fluorescent lighting than it does under tungsten lighting. But variations in color rendering produced by different light sources are not as important as having enough light to see fine details clearly. Although natural light is desirable, tungsten or fluorescent light, or a combination of the two, will do.

The basic tools for process identification are an inexpensive hand-held magnifier and (more importantly for the beginner) a low-power stereomicroscope. Once a certain level of skill has been achieved, most process determination can be made with the unaided eye or with a magnifier.

The most useful magnifiers for process identification are of about 10X magnification and do not need to rest directly on the print to be in focus. "Linen tester" magnifiers, which fold flat when not in use, are of this type, and are available from most printer supply stores. The magnifier is primarily used to distinguish between photographs and images produced on a printing press by photomechanical means, but it can also clearly show binder-layer damage, mold colonies, and other small features.

The microscope, on the other hand, reveals distinguishing features too small to be seen with the eye or magnifier. Paper fibers, surface textures, and the differentiation between the paper support, baryta layer, and binder layer can all be seen at 30X magnification. Microscopes allow for much more accurate process determination than magnifiers, and are especially helpful when one is first learning to identify the various 19th-century print materials. They are also much more comfortable to use and have a wider field of view.

The low-power stereo microscope is the best tool for use in identification of 19th-century photographic prints. Note the extension arm which allows large prints to be examined.

National Archives and Records Administration

Microscopic examination is necessary to apply correctly the systematic approach described in the *IDENTIFICATION GUIDE* in this chapter. Many of the decisive clues to print identification are microscopic, and beginners who do not have access to a microscope may be frustrated in using the *IDENTIFICATION GUIDE*.

The most useful microscopes for process identification are the low-power, stereoscopic type frequently found in biological laboratories. It is helpful if the microscope has a stand with an extension arm so that any part of a print can be examined. An illuminator designed for microscopy—preferably one with a variable intensity control—is also helpful, but a small, high-intensity desk lamp will suffice. No clips or restraints should be used on prints during microscopic examination. A 20X-30X magnification is generally best for identifying processes.

Daguerreotypes may be identified by their highly polished silver surfaces and the fact that at different angles of view, the image appears either as a positive (top) or a negative (bottom left).

Leslie Stroebel

IDENTIFYING DAGUERREOTYPES, AMBROTYPES, AND TINTYPES

This book is limited in scope to 19th-century positive photographic images on paper supports, but a few words on identifying other common types of 19th-century positive images may be in order. A positive image is one in which the subject's actual tonality is correctly rendered; that is, light areas appear light in the image, and dark areas dark. A negative image is one in which the subject's tonalities are reversed, with light areas appearing dark.

Three important types of positive images made during the 19th century did not have paper supports: daguerreotypes, ambrotypes, and tintypes.

DAGUERREOTYPES

Daguerreotypes, popular from the early 1840s until 1860 or so, consist of a positive image on a thin copper plate with a highly polished, mirror-like coating of silver. Daguerreotype plates are quite delicate and liable to tarnish. They were usually placed in a sealed package with a pane of glass to protect the plate from atmospheric and mechanical damage. In America, daguerreotypes were most often placed in small hinged cases made of wood with a leather or paper covering, or in the so-called "union cases" made of a molded thermoplastic material. The daguerreotype's distinguishing features are its highly polished silver support and its quality of appearing either as a negative or a positive depending on the angle of view and the direction from which light falls on it. Daguerreotypes are unique in this respect, and are therefore easy to identify.

AMBROTYPES AND TINTYPES

The other two types of positive images on non-paper supports, *ambrotypes* and *tintypes*, are closely related. Both consist of a positive, physically-developed silver image in a collodion binder on an opaque, non-reflective support. The lightest parts of their images have the most silver; the darkest areas have none, and reveal only the dark, non-reflective support.

In reflected light, these images have a characteristic creamy, whitish appearance because their silver image particles are the right size and shape to scatter some light back to the eye, rather than absorbing the light to make the image appear black. The more silver present in a given area, the whiter the image looks. Only a small amount of light incident on ambrotypes and tintypes is scattered back to the eye, so there is a limit to the brightness of their highlight areas. This limited tonal range is one of the identifying features of these processes.

The two processes essentially differ in their supports: ambrotypes have a glass support, while tintypes have a support made of a thin sheet of lacquered iron.

The ambrotype process was in use from 1855 to about 1865 but enjoyed its greatest popularity in the late 1850s. Several opaque, non-reflective supports were used with ambrotypes, including dark red or purple glass, and clear glass backed with black velvet or black varnish. These supports had to be protected, and most ambrotypes were put in cases like those used for daguerreotypes. Because the ambrotype largely replaced the daguerreotype as the most popular portrait medium, the cases were already available and familiar to the public. Ambrotypes can be identified by the fact that their images appear negative when examined by light *transmitted* through the glass support. Unlike daguerreotypes, which switch from positive to negative depending on the angle at which they are held, the ambrotype "package" must be disassembled and the plate examined by transmitted light for this to happen. The ambrotype normally appears as a positive image no matter what the angle of view. Therefore, it should not be necessary to disassemble an ambrotype in order to identify it.

Tintypes appeared in the late 1850s and were made well into the 20th century. They are easy to identify because of their support, which is actually made of iron. ("Tintype" is therefore a misnomer; other names for the process are "ferrotype" and "melainotype.") Tintypes are harder to identify when placed in cases like those used for daguerreotypes and ambrotypes. Such cases disguise the nature of the support and make a tintype look like an ambrotype. A small, fairly strong magnet held against the center of the glass will reveal whether an image is a tintype.

Several other processes used between 1850 and 1870 were based on the same principle of a positive image in a collodion binder on dark, opaque supports that included black leather, oilcloth, and even black paper. Such images are uncommon.

IDENTIFYING PRINT PROCESSES: THE IDENTIFICATION GUIDE

The *IDENTIFICATION GUIDE* can serve as a vital tool in determining the process identity of a photographic or photomechanical print made before 1900. It is based on an analysis of a series of clues derived from visual and microscopic examination of the print, and consists of three parts: a text explaining the clues (pages 52–68), an organizational flowchart with abbreviated clues (pages 54–55), and a listing of physical descriptions of all the major processes (pages 69–72).

How to Use the IDENTIFICATION GUIDE

To identify a print process using the *IDENTIFICATION GUIDE* first read this entire chapter thoroughly and study the organizational flowchart located inside the back cover of the book. The flowchart summarizes what to look for in examining a print. It is a roadmap which leads the reader from a common starting point at the top, down through and across various levels of clues, to a positive identification of one of the processes listed at right. A photomacrograph is shown for each process. The flowchart is in the form of a "decision tree," in which the choices are successively narrowed until only one alternative is left. At each level of the "tree," it is necessary to decide, based on the visual, microscopic, and surface characteristics of the print, which branch to take. On the reverse side of the flowchart, there are examples of each process accompanied by a photomacrograph of the example plus approximate dates of use.

A glance at the flowchart shows that it has three main levels of decision-making. At the first level, a decision is made as to whether a print is photomechanical or photographic, based on whether or not a *grain pattern* is visible in the image under magnification. Photomechanical prints (with the one exception of the woodburytype) all have some kind of grain pattern, while true photographic prints always have a smooth, continuous transition from lighter to darker tones, with no visible grain pattern.

To help orient the reader, graphic symbols are placed on the flowchart to indicate the basis for key decisions and point the direction to go in. The photomechanical branch of the chart is marked with the symbol:

The continuous tone branch is marked with the symbol:

Appropriate sections of the flowchart also appear in the text which accompanies and explains the *IDENTIFICATION GUIDE* in detail (pages 56–68).

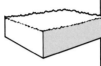

One Layer:
Paper Support

Two Layers:
Binder
and Support

Three Layers:
Binder, Baryta,
and Support

The second level of decision-making involves the layer structure and surface character of the various print processes. These characteristics are of primary importance in distinguishing among the various true photographic processes, but are of less importance in the identification of photomechanical prints. It is necessary to sub-divide the numerous kinds of true photographic prints according to their *layer structure* before narrowing the choices any further. There are three possible layer structures: one layer, two layers, or three layers. These are symbolized on this page. Using magnification together with visual examination, it is not difficult to decide which of the three possible layer structures a given print has.

The third level of decision-making is based on *individual characteristics* of the processes. These are features such as color, typical forms of deterioration, characteristic grain patterns, etc. It is at this level that a positive determination of process identity can be made.

> Therefore, to summarize, a print process is identified by first looking for a *grain pattern*, then determining the *layer structure*, and finally by recognizing *individual characteristics*. At every level of the flowchart, the clues (things to look for) are coded to tell the reader whether to examine the print visually, to use magnification, or to examine the print's surface character.

The text on pages 56–68 takes the reader through the flowchart in step-by-step fashion, explaining in detail exactly what to look for. Once a tentative process identification has been made, the last step is to double-check whether all the characteristics of the print in question match up with those given in the alphabetical *Summary of Physical Descriptions* found on pages 69–72. Here such things as approximate dates of use, relevant physical characteristics, typical forms of deterioration, and common formats are listed in one place for easy reference.

BEFORE BEGINNING: SOME POINTS TO REMEMBER

The *IDENTIFICATION GUIDE* is designed for novices and those with an intermediate level of expertise. It allows for process identification of most types of 19th-century prints, but it is by necessity a simplification. Some images are hybrids of processes mentioned in the *GUIDE*, and others were made by processes too rare or unusual to be given a place in it. In using the *GUIDE*, it is well to remember Hamlet's admonition: "There are more things in Heaven and earth, Horatio, than are dreamt of in your philosophy."

Though the *IDENTIFICATION GUIDE* will almost always lead to a correct process determination, it cannot take the place of a trained photographic conservation specialist or curator when an expert opinion is required.

Two points need to be considered before using the *IDENTIFICATION GUIDE* on a print:

1) Decide whether the print is photographically generated or a drawing of some sort. The *GUIDE* is only appropriate for camera-originated images. Realistic rendering of detail, the perspective created by a camera lens, and the lack of obvious cross-hatching to create shading all suggest the photographic origin of an image.

2) Make every effort to accurately date the print. If some clue— an inscribed date, a datable clue like a car in the image, or any other evidence— suggests that the print was made after 1900, use the *IDENTIFICATION GUIDE* cautiously or not at all. (Bear in mind that many old images have been copied onto modern materials, so that even datable clues may not establish when a particular print was made.)

The GUIDE may be misleading when used with prints made after 1900 utilizing newer photographic materials and photomechanical processes. Its cut-off point is inevitably somewhat arbitrary because many of the processes included in the *GUIDE* were used during the present century. However, the proliferation of new processes and materials after 1900 makes it risky to use the *GUIDE* with 20th-century prints.

The most effective way to master the *IDENTIFICATION GUIDE* is to use it with known examples of the various processes. Labeled examples were often included in advertisements in such 19th-century photographic journals as *The Philadelphia Photographer* and *Anthony's Photographic Bulletin*.

FLOWCHART FOR IDENTIFICATION GUIDE

From Care and Identification of
19th-Century Photographic Prints
by James M. Reilly

How To Use The Flowchart
Choose Between Photomechanical and True Photograph
For True Photographs, Choose One-, Two-, or Three-Layer Structure, Then Choose Individual Characteristics

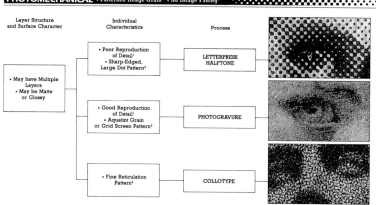

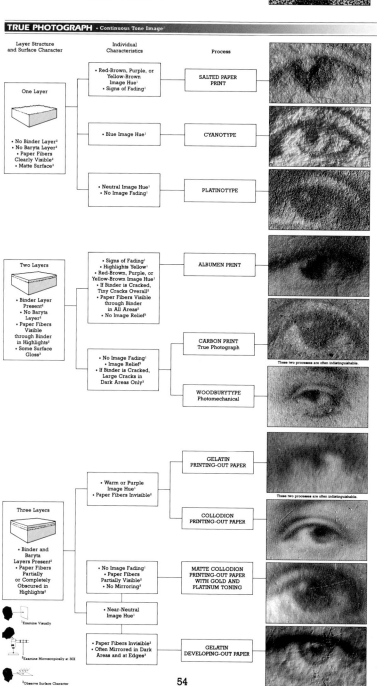

Organizational flowchart for *IDENTIFICATION GUIDE* to 19th-century photographic and photomechanical prints. The full-size flowchart can be found inside the back cover. Extra copies of the organizational flowchart (KODAK Publication No. G-2Sa) are available.

MAJOR 19TH-CENTURY PHOTOGRAPHIC AND PHOTOMECHANICAL PROCESSES

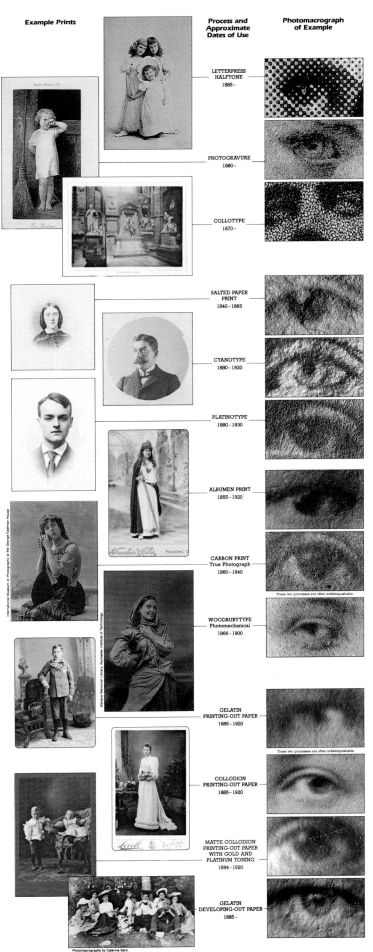

Example Prints	Process and Approximate Dates of Use	Photomacrograph of Example
	LETTERPRESS HALFTONE 1885–	
	PHOTOGRAVURE 1880–	
	COLLOTYPE 1870–	
	SALTED PAPER PRINT 1840–1865	
	CYANOTYPE 1880–1920	
	PLATINOTYPE 1880–1930	
	ALBUMEN PRINT 1855–1920	
	CARBON PRINT True Photograph 1860–1940	
	WOODBURYTYPE Photomechanical 1866–1900	These two processes are often indistinguishable.
	GELATIN PRINTING-OUT PAPER 1885–1920	These two processes are often indistinguishable.
	COLLODION PRINTING-OUT PAPER 1885–1920	
	MATTE COLLODION PRINTING-OUT PAPER WITH GOLD AND PLATINUM TONING 1894–1920	
	GELATIN DEVELOPING-OUT PAPER 1885–	

Photomacrographs by Caterina Salvi.
All Other Photos Courtesy of James M. Reilly

Reverse side of the flowchart shows examples of the major 19th-century photographic and photomechanical print processes with their approximate dates of use.

M5G043
KODAK Publication No. G-2Sa
©Eastman Kodak Company, 1986

Photographic Products Group
EASTMAN KODAK COMPANY • ROCHESTER, NY 14650
Printed in the United States of America

Kodak is a trademark.

- May have Multiple
  Layers
- May be Matte
  or Glossy

- Poor Reproduction
  of Detail¹
- Sharp-Edged,
  Large Dot Pattern²

LETTERPRESS
HALFTONE

THE KEY QUESTION: PATTERNED IMAGE GRAIN OR CONTINUOUS TONE?

To use the *IDENTIFICATION GUIDE* with a given print, begin by examining the image with a hand-held 10X magnifier or, preferably, a low-power stereomicroscope. Examine a middletone area first.

A simple determination needs to be made at this point. Does the image have the completely gradual change from gray to black that is characteristic of photographic prints? Or does it have a grain pattern that breaks flat tonal areas into lines, dots, or an irregular stipple of some kind? Look for any type of grain or screen pattern which suggests that the image was photomechanically printed. Use the photomicrographic illustrations of each process given below as a guide in deciding whether there is a grain pattern.

If no detectable grain pattern is present and the progression of tones from light to dark is smooth and continuous, the print is likely to be a true photograph. Another indication that a print is a true photograph may be the presence of localized or generalized image fading. Photomechanical prints may be stained but they do not fade.

PHOTOMECHANICAL PRINTS: IMAGES WITH A GRAIN PATTERN

The presence of some kind of grain or dot pattern indicates that an image was produced on a printing press by photomechanical means. Don't be confused by the coloration of the print; virtually any image color can be rendered in photomechanically reproduced prints.

Although many photomechanical processes were used during the 19th century, the *GUIDE* deals only with the three most important: letterpress halftone, photogravure, and collotype. To identify a photomechanical process, examine the print under the microscope at 30X magnification. The grain pattern should comfortably fall into one of these three categories.

Letterpress Halftones: Sharp-Edged, Regular Dots

Letterpress halftones are the easiest of the photomechanical processes to identify. They have relatively large

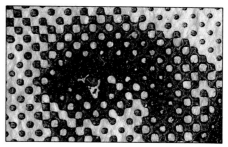

Relatively poor reproduction of detail and large, sharp-edged dots are characteristics of *letterpress halftones* made in the 19th century. An enlarged portion at 30X magnification shows how ink has been squeezed from the centers of the dots.

James M. Reilly
Photomacrograph,
Caterina Salvi

dots which in a middle-gray area resemble a checkerboard of sharp-edged squares. Small circular dots are seen in light areas, and the ink film in dark areas is solid except for small, unprinted circles.

Letterpress halftones are printed from a relief plate, and therefore often have a ridge of ink along the edges of the dots where the ink was squeezed out by the pressure of the plate against the paper. The dot centers have less ink and may even have spaces where ink was entirely squeezed away. Their sharply defined edges are the most distinctive aspect of letterpress-halftone dots. Other photomechanical printing processes based on a screen pattern produce softer, less defined dots. Nineteenth-century halftones typically had too large a screen ruling (or dot size) to reproduce fine details well; their dot pattern can often be seen with the unaided eye. Any typographic matter printed with letterpress halftones is usually crisply rendered, with sharp, unbroken edges and a squeezed-out ridge of ink outlining the letters.

Photogravures: Fine Detail, Variable Ink Deposit, and Aquatint Grain

Photogravures are made by an intaglio process from a plate with tiny etched pits which, during printing, are filled according to their depth with greater or lesser amounts of ink. Tonal gradations in photogravure are produced by varying the amounts of ink on the page, and not, as with letterpress halftones and collotypes, by always printing the maximum amount of ink and only varying the area covered. Therefore, one of the distinguishing characteristics of photogravures under microscopic examination is a variation in the amount of ink deposited: less in light areas and more in dark areas.

If one is not sure whether a print is a photogravure or collotype, the light highlight areas can provide a clue. Photogravure highlights are lightly printed; collotype highlights are fine, threadlike lines or elongated spots of deep, intense color.

The fact that ink is deposited in varying amounts suggests that photogravures might be hard to distinguish from photographic images, since both use continually varying amounts of image material to produce tonal variations. Photogravures, however,

En Penitence

• May have Multiple Layers
• May be Matte or Glossy

• Good Reproduction of Detail[1]
• Aquatint Grain or Grid Screen Pattern[2]

PHOTOGRAVURE

Photogravures have a fine, irregular pattern known as an aquatint grain (see 30X enlargement) which allows for excellent reproduction of detail.

James M. Reilly
Photomacrograph,
Caterina Salvi

• Good Reproduction
of Detail[1]
• Aquatint Grain
or Grid Screen Pattern[2]

PHOTOGRAVURE

A late 19th-century innovation in photomechanical reproduction was rotary photogravure, in which the printing plate was a copper cylinder. An enlarged area at 30X magnification reveals a pattern of intersecting white lines.

James M. Reilly
Photomacrograph,
Caterina Salvi

have a fine, irregular grain pattern that real photographs lack. This pattern is produced by dusting the plate with rosin, a technique borrowed from the much older aquatint process. While its size varies, the "aquatint" pattern is usually visible with a hand-held magnifier.

Close examination of a textured highlight area of a photogravure at 30X magnification will clearly show that the image is broken up into an irregular grain pattern. The ink deposit in a photogravure will have a speckled appearance. It seems to rest on the surface of the paper fibers, and not to penetrate and stain them, as is the case in a binderless photograph such as a salted paper print. The small grain size possible in photogravures reproduces fine detail very successfully. Some photogravures— usually those printed in large editions from rotary cylinders rather than flat plates—have a grid-like screen pattern similar to that produced by a halftone screen. The dots in screened photogravures are soft-edged, and are usually too small to be seen with the naked eye.

Other clues to the identity of photogravures are the presence of a plate mark and a characteristic rendering of any typographic matter which may accompany the image. Photogravures made from flat plates were printed under great pressure to ensure that all the ink was withdrawn from the etched cells of the plate. This pressure created a plate mark on the paper—an embossed line around the edges of the plate, usually at some distance from the image. But the absence or presence of a plate mark cannot of itself positively identify the process by which a print was made: plate marks were trimmed off some photogravures, and artificial plate marks were sometimes embossed on other, less expensive kinds of prints to emulate the appearance of a photo-gravure.

Typographic matter accompanying a gravure print will not have sharply defined edges because the aquatint grain is present on all areas of the plate and does not reproduce the thin lines and serifs of type well. Some photogravure plates were "enhanced" by engravers who used traditional hand engraving techniques to darken shadows and outline forms. Such work is very apparent under the microscope as even, hard-edged dark lines.

Collotypes: Fine Detail, Reticulated Grain Pattern

The collotype process was extremely versatile and could be used on almost any type of paper surface, smooth or rough. Collotypes are easiest to identify by the unique shape of their grain pattern, known as *reticulation* and created when a gelatin layer is oven-dried and then swollen rapidly in cool water so that the surface spontaneously fractures into a network of fissures. This reticulated gelatin layer is actually used to print the image. The reticulation controls the amount of ink accepted or rejected by the gelatin layer.

At 30X magnification, the reticulation pattern in lighter middletones makes the collotype image seem to be broken up into a mosaic of irregularly-shaped but uniformly-sized cells. The fineness of the reticulation may vary from print to print but is never large enough to be visible with the naked eye. In highlight areas the image is composed of dark, thread-like lines of ink. Ink may completely cover the shadow areas. Collotypes are sometimes accompanied by type matter printed by other methods such as letterpress, or by a non-reticulated variant of the collotype process. No indentation or plate mark is created by a collotype impression.

The collotype process produced excellent, detailed reproductions of photographic images. It was less expensive to produce large editions of collotype reproductions than to produce a large number of platinotypes or albumen prints. Collotype's high quality and versatility made it the favorite of publishers who wanted a photomechanical process to closely mimic the appearance of actual photographs. Collotypes were some-

times used to copy photographs with uncanny precision (and, presumably, to bring a comparable price). The best of these copies were done with remarkable skill. Imitation platinotypes were printed in gray-black ink on matte papers, and imitation silver prints were done on smooth paper and coated with a glaze of gelatin or a similar substance. Inks were chosen to resemble closely the colors of albumen prints and of gelatin and collodion printing-out papers. Even imitation photogravures were made by the collotype process. In all of these cases, the reticulation pattern will establish the print as a collotype.

IN THE POET'S CORNER

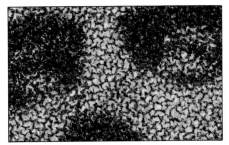

The outstanding feature of the *collotype* process is the irregular grain pattern known as *reticulation* readily visible in this 30X enlargement.

James M. Reilly Photomacrograph, Caterina Salvi

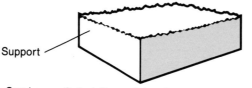

Support

One-Layer: Salted Paper Print, Cyanotype, Platinotype

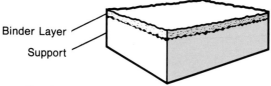

Binder Layer

Support

Two-Layers: Albumen Print, Woodburytype, Carbon Print

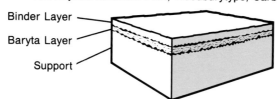

Binder Layer

Baryta Layer

Support

Three-Layers: Gelatin and Collodion Printing-Out Papers,
Gelatin Developing-Out Papers

Shown here is a schematic drawing of the three layer structures found in 19th-century photographic print materials.

TRUE PHOTOGRAPHIC PRINTS: CONTINUOUS-TONE IMAGES

Choosing Between a One-, Two-, or Three-Layer Structure

An image with no discernible grain pattern is probably a true photographic print. There are quite a few kinds of photographic prints, so the range of possibilities must first be narrowed by analyzing the layer structure and surface character of the print to decide which of the three broad branches of the chart they fall under. Both visual and microscopic examination will be needed to make these distinctions.

There are three possible layer structures for a 19th-century photographic print. These are shown in the accompanying sketch. The simplest structure is that of a plain, uncoated sheet of paper. The most important clue to prints of this type is that the surface is matte, with no gloss or sheen. Under the microscope, individual paper fibers are clearly visible in all areas of the print. This simple, binderless structure is the easiest to identify.

The second possible structure has two components: the paper support and a *binder*, a coating of a transparent material which contains the image. When a binder layer is present, the surface character of the print changes and usually there is a gloss or sheen. The best way to decide if a print is matte or glossy is to examine it visually from several angles, tilting it

back and forth to explore the surface character. The amount of glossiness can vary, but a slight sheen or any noticeable difference from the appearance of an uncoated sheet of paper indicates the presence of a binder.

More information, however, is needed before deciding which of the two remaining branches of the chart to take. This is because the third possible structure also has a binder layer, and the surface character of both types of prints can be quite similar.

The next key question is whether the print has a baryta layer under the transparent binder layer. A baryta layer is a coating of white-pigmented gelatin which covers the paper support like the icing on a cake, forming a smooth, reflective substrate for the binder layer.

To check for a baryta layer, examine a highlight or a light-middletone area under the microscope at 30X magnification. If there is a baryta layer, the fibers of the paper support will not be clearly visible because the baryta is opaque and obscures the fibers. Some baryta coatings are thick and smooth; others are thinner and allow a hint of the fiber contours to show.

If no baryta layer is present, individual paper fibers will be clearly visible through the transparent binder, at least in highlight and light-middletone areas. If you can clearly distinguish individual paper fibers, the photographic print does not have a baryta coating.

Salted Paper Print

Albumen Print

The appearance of photographic prints at 42X magnification depends on their layer structure. A salted paper print (top left) has only one layer—its paper support with no coatings. In an albumen print (top right), the paper fibers can be seen through a transparent binder layer. In matte collodion printing-out paper (lower left), there is a thinly coated baryta layer between the support and the binder. In glossy collodion printing-out paper (lower right), the baryta layer is thick and smooth, completely covering up the fibers of the support. Note how passage through a burnishing machine has folded back the corners of the binder layers.

Photomacrographs, Caterina Salvi

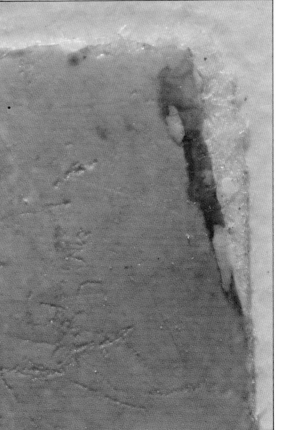

Matte Collodion Printing-Out Paper

Glossy Collodion Printing-Out Paper

One Layer

• No Binder Layer[1]
• No Baryta Layer[1]
• Paper Fibers Clearly Visible[1]
• Matte Surface[1]

• Red-Brown, Purple, or Yellow-Brown Image Hue[1]
• Signs of Fading[1]

SALTED PAPER PRINT

• Blue Image Hue[1]

CYANOTYPE

• Neutral Image Hue[1]
• No Image Fading[1]

PLATINOTYPE

Prints with a Simple One-Layer Structure: Matte Surface, No Binder, No Baryta, Paper Fibers Clearly Visible

If under visual and microscopic examination the print surface looks like an uncoated book page: that is, it has no baryta coating or binder layer, and the tangled paper fibers are clearly visible, the photograph was most likely made by one of three processes distinguishable by the color and character of the image. When magnified, the middletone areas of these prints seem evenly to stain or dye the paper fibers, unlike ink images which seem to rest entirely on the paper surface as isolated, shining encrustations.

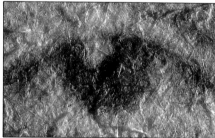

Warm image hues and signs of image fading are characteristic of *salted paper prints*. Under the microscope at 30X, the image appears to "stain" the uppermost paper fibers.

James M. Reilly Photomacrograph, Caterina Salvi

Salted Paper Prints

If the image is reddish-brown, purple or yellow-brown, it is likely to be a *salted paper print*. Salted paper prints usually show signs of image fading that can include variations in image color, edge fading, small yellow spots, and lack of highlight detail. If in doubt as to whether an image is a salted paper print or a platinotype, see if the subject matter suggests the image's date of origin. Although salted paper prints enjoyed a modest revival in the 1890s, they were most popular from 1840 to about 1855, well before the discovery and subsequent popularity of the platinotype during the 1880s and '90s.

The blue image hue of *cyanotypes* makes them easy to identify. They normally do not fade if kept in the dark. The fibers of the support are plainly visible at 30X magnification.

James M. Reilly Photomacrograph, Caterina Salvi

Cyanotypes

If the image is a bright, uniform blue, the print is a *cyanotype.*

Platinotypes

If the image is neutral black or a warm, brownish-black and no image fading is observable, the image is probably a *platinotype*. Before deciding that it is, look for the two forms of deterioration associated with platinotypes: the catalytic "transfer image" phenomenon (described in Chapter II) and deterioration in the primary support.

Platinotypes have a matte surface and delicate tonality. Their image color is generally black, sometimes with a bluish cast. At 30X magnification, their surface character is similar to salted paper prints.

James M. Reilly Photomacrograph, Caterina Salvi

Prints with a Two-Layer Structure: Binder Present, No Baryta Layer

If under visual examination a shiny coating shows on the print surface, and under microscopic examination no baryta layer is found and paper fibers are visible in highlight areas, the print is one of three types: albumen print, carbon print, or woodburytype. While it may be difficult to distinguish a carbon print from a woodburytype, there are a number of ways in which to make a positive identification of an albumen print.

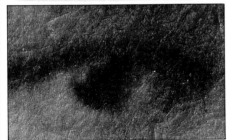

Highlight yellowing, image fading, and warm image colors typify *albumen prints.* Paper fibers may be seen through the albumen layer, even in the darkest shadow areas, at 30X magnification.

James M. Reilly Photomacrograph, Caterina Salvi

Albumen Prints

A crucial clue to the identity of albumen prints is the presence of some form of localized or overall image fading. Unfaded albumen prints are purplish-brown or purple, and usually have good highlight detail. Signs of image fading are nearly always present in albumen prints, and may include a yellowish-red image color, overall lightness and loss of highlight detail, yellow spots, fading at edges, blotchiness, and silver mirroring. Any image fading will rule out the possibility that a print is a carbon print or woodburytype because they have pigment images and usually do not fade.

The surface of an albumen print may range from slightly glossy to very glossy. The surface character will be completely uniform, and no relief effect will be present (for an explanation of the relief effect, see *Carbon Prints* and *Woodburytypes* pages 64-65). The albumen layer may have a network of tiny cracks and fissures in either a parallel or random orientation. These cracks may be just large enough to see with the naked eye, or may only be visible upon careful microscopic examination. Not all albumen prints have these tiny cracks, but many do.

Another common characteristic of albumen prints is the tendency for the albumen coating to turn yellow, giving the highlights a yellow or yellowish-brown appearance. While not all albumen prints have yellow highlights, the phenomenon is much more common in albumen prints than in other print types. Yellowing is rare in carbon prints and woodburytypes.

Because albumen prints have no baryta layer, individual paper fibers are visible through the albumen binder during microscopic examination. The fibers are clearly discernible even in the very darkest shadow areas of albumen prints. This is not the case with carbon prints and woodburytypes, in which the gelatin binder in shadow areas contains so much pigment that it becomes opaque and obscures the paper fibers.

Two Layers

• Binder Layer Present[2]
• No Baryta Layer[2]
• Paper Fibers Visible through Binder in Highlights[2]
• Some Surface Gloss[2]

• Signs of Fading[1]
• Highlights Yellow[1]
• Red-Brown, Purple, or Yellow-Brown Image Hue[1]
• If Binder is Cracked, Tiny Cracks Overall[2]
• Paper Fibers Visible through Binder in All Areas[2]
• No Image Relief[2]

ALBUMEN PRINT

Two Layers

• Binder Layer
Present²
• No Baryta
Layer²
• Paper Fibers
Visible
through Binder
in Highlights²
• Some Surface
Gloss³

• No Image Fading¹
• Image Relief³
• If Binder is Cracked,
Large Cracks in
Dark Areas Only³

CARBON PRINT
True Photograph

Carbon Prints

Both carbon prints and woodbury-types exhibit two outstanding characteristics: they can be of any image color, and they display no image fading of any kind. Their images seem remarkably well preserved in comparison to the usual faded condition of albumen prints. The image color of 19th-century carbon prints and woodburytypes will often be quite close to that of a well-preserved albumen print because a conscious attempt was made to simulate albumen prints by blending pigments to achieve a purplish-brown image hue.

The other characteristic useful in identifying a carbon print is the varying thickness of its gelatin binder layer in the light and dark areas of the image. In deep shadow areas, there is a thick deposit of pigmented gelatin; but in the highlights, there is only a thin deposit or none at all. This difference gives rise to the "image relief effect."

To determine if a print has an image relief, examine it from a low angle with specular illumination (that is, hold the print between the eye and the light source, and tilt the print so that the "glare" from the print surface is most noticeable). A relief effect will be most obvious along boundaries between very light and very dark areas, such as the collar line of a man wearing a dark suit and a white shirt. Any difference in the surface reflection at such a boundary indicates that a print is a carbon print or woodbury-type. Other print types have a uniform binder layer in all areas of the print and therefore show no relief effect. The image relief of carbon prints can be quite subtle, however, and it may not always be possible to use this characteristic to identify them.

The gelatin binders of both carbon prints and woodburytypes sometimes develop a pattern of large cracks that is easily visible to the naked eye. Such cracking has a random mosaic orientation and is confined to dark areas of the print where the gelatin binder is thickest. One final characteristic useful in identifying carbon prints and woodburytypes is the presence of undispersed specks of pigment, visible at 30X magnification in dark-middle-tone areas. Undispersed pigment appears as varying-sized specks of deep color. Sometimes the specks are of different colors that reveal how the image hue was achieved by blending pigments. Most, but not all, carbon prints and woodburytypes have pigment specks.

The pigments used in the *carbon print* can be of any color and usually do not fade. Under the microscope at 30X, paper fibers are visible only in highlight and middle-tone areas. Specks of undispersed pigment are evident in this example.

IMP/GEH
Photomacrograph,
Caterina Salvi

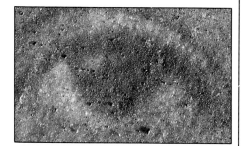

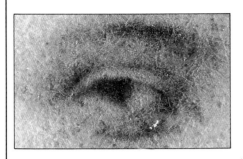

Woodburytypes

It is difficult, if not impossible, to tell woodburytypes from carbon prints because they are essentially the same kind of object: a pigment image in a gelatin binder which varies in thickness according to the lightness or darkness of the print. Therefore, the essential characteristics of the carbon print—no fading, an image relief, and the possibility of being printed in any color—are also those of the woodburytype. The difference between carbon prints and woodburytypes lies in how they were made. The carbon print is a true photographic print because it was once light-sensitive. Each one was exposed to a negative and "developed" in warm water. Woodburytypes are not photograph-

ic prints at all, but photomechanical. They were made on a special printing press using pigmented gelatin as "ink."

In spite of the basic similarity between carbon prints and woodburytypes, there are a few clues (none of them infallible) which may help differentiate the two processes. Woodburytypes usually appear to have a more prominent image relief than carbon prints. Woodburytypes are usually small, and never larger than 11 x 14 inches (28.6 x 36.2 cm), whereas fairly large carbon prints are not uncommon. Most woodburytypes were produced as book illustrations and labeled as such. Those of French origin may be labeled "Photoglyptie."

Woodburytypes are photomechanical prints that have no grain pattern. They can be of any image color, and do not fade. At 30X magnification, paper fibers are apparent primarily in highlight and middletone areas.

Wallace Memorial Library, Rochester Institute of Technology

Photomacrograph, Caterina Salvi

Like carbon prints, woodburytypes have an image "relief effect," where shadow areas are glossier and more elevated than highlight areas. There is also a tendency in both materials for large cracks to appear in the shadow areas as shown in the detail at right, illuminated with raking light.

IMP/GEH

Prints With Warm Image Colors

Prints With Near-Neutral Image Colors

The descriptors
"warm" and "near-
neutral" appear in the
*IDENTIFICATION
GUIDE* and are meant
to describe a family of
possible image colors.
These sample prints
are only intended to
suggest the range of
hues involved.

James M. Reilly

Prints with a Three-Layer Structure: Binder and Baryta Layer Present, Paper Fibers Partially or Completely Obscured in Highlights

The confirmation of the presence of a baryta layer is an important piece of information. Prints with the three-part support/baryta/binder structure date from after 1885. Included in this group are both printing-out and developing-out papers. Clues from both visual and microscopic examination are needed to tell them apart.

Begin to narrow the range of possibilities by analyzing the image color and classifying it either as "very warm" (red, reddish-brown or purple) or "near-neutral" (greenish- or neutral black). This determination is important because (with one notable exception) it distinguishes printing-out papers from developing-out papers. The terms "warm" and "near-neutral" are not meant to describe precise shades but rather two ranges or families of colors. Since it is nearly impossible to define a range of colors using only words, the accompanying illustration attempts to convey visually what is meant by "warm image colors" and "near-neutral image colors."

Anyone who has seen an ordinary black-and-white photographic print will have some sense of a "near-neutral image hue." Experienced photographers know that not all black-and-white prints are neutral black. Some have a greenish or blue-black cast, while others are a brownish-black. The term "near-neutral image hue" is meant to encompass the entire range of "blacks" possible with black-and-white photographic prints.

The term "warm image hues" is meant to describe the range of colors found in silver printing-out papers. This is a somewhat wider range of colors that extends from brick red through chocolate brown, purplish-brown, and on to a rich bluish-purple. A print whose color is within this range of hues is probably on some type of printing-out paper. Such prints normally remain within the "warm" range of image hues as they deteriorate, but advanced sulfiding deterioration can result in a yellow-green or greenish-brown color in most kinds of printing-out papers, including albumen prints.

Three Layers

• Binder and
Baryta
Layers Present²
• Paper Fibers
Partially
or Completely
Obscured in
Highlights²

• Warm or Purple
Image Hue¹
• Paper Fibers Invisible²

GELATIN
PRINTING-OUT PAPER

COLLODION
PRINTING-OUT PAPER

Gelatin printing-out paper somewhat resembles an albumen print because of its brown or purple image color. However, at 30X magnification, it can be easily distinguished from albumen by the presence of a smooth baryta layer which hides all traces of paper fibers.

James M. Reilly
Photomacrograph,
Caterina Salvi

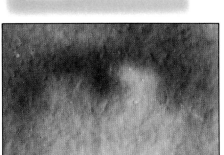

Glossy collodion printing-out paper (30X magnification, bottom) differs from gelatin printing-out paper only in subtle nuances of image color. The two processes are virtually indistinguishable since both have purple-brown image hues and a smooth print surface.

James M. Reilly
Photomacrograph,
Caterina Salvi

Warm Image Hues: Gelatin or Collodion Printing-Out Papers

Warm image hues indicate that a print is either gelatin printing-out paper or collodion printing-out paper. These materials look so much alike that they are virtually indistinguishable, and in most cases it will not be possible to tell them apart using only visual and microscopic examination. However, for most preservation or curatorial purposes it is sufficient to leave the identity of the binder material unresolved and simply identify them as "silver printing-out papers."

Near-Neutral Image Hues

A black, olive-black, brown-black, or slightly bluish-black image hue does not in and of itself provide sufficient information to identify the paper used for a print. Two possible print materials have a near-neutral image color: gelatin developing-out paper, and matte collodion printing-out paper toned with gold and platinum. Both materials were popular at the very end of the 19th century and beginning of the 20th century. A combination of clues from visual and microscopic examinations can be used to tell them apart.

Three Layers

• Binder and
Baryta
Layers Present²
• Paper Fibers
Partially
or Completely
Obscured in
Highlights²

• Near-Neutral
Image Hue¹

• No Image Fading¹
• Paper Fibers
Partially Visible²
• No Mirroring³

MATTE COLLODION
PRINTING-OUT PAPER
WITH GOLD AND
PLATINUM TONING

• Paper Fibers Invisible²
• Often Mirrored in Dark
Areas and at Edges³

GELATIN
DEVELOPING-OUT PAPER

Matte Collodion Printing-Out Papers Toned With Gold and Platinum

The most important clue to the identity of this material is the nature of its baryta coating. The baryta layer is quite thin, and the print surface has a distinctive appearance at 30X magnification. Some individual fibers are readily discernible, and the paper texture is partly preserved in the contours and outlines of fibers seen within the baryta coating. The surface character is *midway* between the complete smoothness of the glossy baryta papers (in which no fibers are visible) and the rough tangle of fibers seen in the uncoated, binderless materials like platinum prints and cyanotypes.

Most 19th-century *gelatin developing-out papers* (black-and-white prints) now exhibit some signs of deterioration, such as silver mirroring or a shift from a neutral black color toward yellowish-brown. Under microscopic examination at 30X magnification, the surface of the print is moderately smooth and no paper fibers can be seen.

James M. Reilly
Photomacrograph,
Caterina Salvi

The near-neutral image hue of matte collodion prints results from successive toning treatments in gold and platinum toning baths. These toning treatments imparted excellent resistance to fading, and a helpful characteristic in identifying such prints is the fact that they display little or no image fading and are not affected by silver mirroring. Matte collodion printing-out papers toned with gold and platinum also have very little tendency toward highlight yellowing. They are generally in an excellent state of preservation, but are prone to surface abrasion.

Gelatin Developing-Out Papers

Gelatin developing-out papers (or "black-and-white" papers) are, of course, quite common in photographic collections, as they were the dominant photographic print medium from

around 1905 until about 1960. Examples from the 19th century are less common, but are still numerous. There are two important clues to their identity apart from their near-neutral black image color: a relatively thick baryta coating and the frequent presence of silver mirroring.

The baryta coating of gelatin developing-out papers, either with glossy or matte surface finish, is typically thick enough to hide all traces of paper fibers during microscopic examination. They can be distinguished in this way from matte collodion printing-out papers, which have a thinner baryta coating that allows the outlines of fibers to be seen

Gelatin developing-out papers typically have some signs of image deterioration, most often silver mirroring which appears as a bluish, metallic sheen in shadow areas. To check for mirroring, view the print from a low angle, holding it between the light source and the eye, so that a direct "glare" is achieved. Silver mirroring is usually most severe at the print edges. Other signs of image deterioration may also be present.

A cautionary note: some gelatin developing-out papers were toned with sulfur to achieve a brown or "sepia" image hue. This practice did not become common until well after 1900. Sepia-toned developing-out prints display no image fading or silver mirroring, and usually contain some clue to their 20th-century origin.

An absence of fading and a near-neutral black image color are characteristic of *matte collodion printing-out paper* toned with gold and platinum. Under the microscope at 30X magnification, paper fibers are partially visible, but not nearly so apparent as they would be in an albumen print.

James M. Reilly
Photomacrograph,
Caterina Salvi

SUMMARY OF PHYSICAL DESCRIPTIONS OF THE MAJOR 19TH-CENTURY PHOTOGRAPHIC AND PHOTOMECHANICAL PRINT PROCESSES

This section summarizes the attributes of each of the major 19th-century print types. It should be used for verification once a preliminary identification for a print has been made. It includes approximate dates of use, visual and microscopic characteristics, typical styles of mounts and formats, and characteristic forms of deterioration for each process. The processes are presented in alphabetical order.

ALBUMEN PAPERS

Used early 1850s to 1920, and the dominant print material from 1855 to 1895. Surface slightly glossy to very glossy, with a very thin paper support. Image color ranges from warm reddish-brown to purple-brown, purple and almost black. Usually yellowed in non-image areas. Microscopic examination shows the lack of a baryta layer, with paper fibers clearly visible in highlight areas through the transparent albumen layer. Cracking and fissuring are often present in the albumen binder. Image has continuous tone. Albumen prints were almost always adhered to a secondary support to prevent the curling of the thin primary support.

Albumen prints were the dominant medium for commercial portraiture, 1860–1895. Commercial portraits are found in two principal formats, the *carte de visite* (mount size: $2^3/_8$ x $3^7/_8$ in., or 6 x 10 cm) and the cabinet card (mount size: $4^1/_4$ x $6^1/_2$ in., or 10.8 x 16.6 cm). Virtually all cartes de visite are albumen prints, as are the majority of stereo views.

Image deterioration is almost always present in albumen prints. Characteristic deterioration includes localized fading, a change of image color toward yellow-brown, and loss of highlight detail. Non-image areas may have a faint pink, purple, or blue cast from the presence of dyes added to the albumen binder. The dyes may show local or overall fading.

CARBON PRINTS

Used late 1860s to 1940s. Surface can be matte or glossy, and virtually any image color is possible. Carbon prints have a subtle (but sometimes quite noticeable) relief effect when viewed at a low angle with specular illumination. The relief appears as a difference in surface character related to the lightness or darkness of the image, and is best observed along edges between light and dark areas. Under microscopic examination, the image is found to have continuous tone, and small specks of undispersed pigment are usually present. Paper fibers are most likely visible in non-image and highlight areas, but may be obscured in dark middletones and shadow areas by the pigmented gelatin binder.

The image stability of carbon prints is excellent, and they typically display a completely uniform image color with no sign of image deterioration. When present, deterioration is generally in the form of large cracks in the gelatin binder layer, especially in shadow areas. Carbon prints were often used for book illustration, large-sized topographical views, and for commercial portraiture in a variety of formats, including some cartes de visite and cabinet cards. Most carbon prints were adhered to some form of secondary support.

COLLODION PRINTING-OUT PAPERS

See *Glossy Collodion Printing-Out Papers* or *Matte Collodion Printing-Out Papers*.

COLLOTYPES

Made by a photomechanical reproduction process discovered in the late 1850s and still used for the highest quality reproduction. During the 19th century, the process was used widely for book illustration and for mass publication of topographical views. Collotypes can be found in a variety of surface finishes from matte to very glossy. They may be of any image color and often are very successful imitations of actual photographic processes, such as albumen prints and platinum prints. Although they may have stained or discolored supports, or even an overall yellowed appearance, collotypes will not display image fading.

The outstanding characteristic of all collotypes is the presence of a particular grain pattern called *reticulation*. This pattern, under microscopic examination, is distinctive enough to establish conclusively the identity of the process. The reticulation pattern is usually too small to be seen with the naked eye and consists of a series of irregularly-shaped cells. In highlight areas, the ink deposit is in threadlike curved or jagged lines. In middletone areas, the cells are defined by somewhat thicker walls, and in the deepest shadows, the ink deposit is solid and completely covers the page. Collotype inks tend to be slightly glossier than photogravure inks, a difference most evident in the shadows. No platemark or indentation is made by a collotype impression. "Lichtdruck" and "Albertype" were synonyms for the collotype process.

CYANOTYPES

Only occasionally produced during the period 1840-1880. Most examples originate from the late 1880s to 1920. Cyanotypes have a matte surface and a bright uniform blue image color. The image stability of cyanotypes is good, and severe fading is uncommon. Under microscopic examination, the print surface is identical to an uncoated book page. The image has continuous tone and appears to exist as a blue stain deep in the paper fibers. Characteristic forms of deterioration are staining and embrittlement of the primary support. Because no binder is present, curl is not a problem for cyanotypes and many are unmounted. Little commercial portraiture was done with cyanotypes; most 19th-century examples are the work of amateurs.

GELATIN DEVELOPING-OUT PAPERS

Used mid-1880s to the present day. Became widely used only during and after the late 1890s. Surfaces may be matte or glossy, and have near-neutral image colors. Silver mirroring is usually present in shadow areas. When examined under the microscope, no paper fibers are visible because they are completely covered by the baryta layer. From 1885 to 1895, some bromide developing-out papers were produced which had no baryta layer; nearly all surviving ex-

amples of this type display very heavy silver mirroring.

Characteristic forms of deterioration include yellowing and fading of the lighter image tones, and overall fading. Advanced sulfiding deterioration due to retained thiosulfate imparts a faded, greenish-black or yellowish-green appearance. During the 19th century, gelatin developing-out papers were used by professional photographers for making enlargements; in the last years of the century, they were used by amateur photographers for contact-printing snapshots. Developing-out papers were not widely used for commercial portraiture until after 1905.

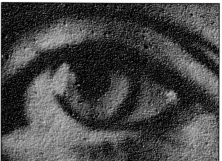

To achieve a matte surface on *gelatin developing-out papers*, substances such as starch, silica, or resins were added to the gelatin emulsion. The presence of these "matting agents" can easily be seen at 30X magnification.

James M. Reilly
Photomacrograph,
Caterina Salvi

GELATIN PRINTING-OUT PAPERS

Used late 1880s to 1920s. The surface character of 19th-century examples is usually quite glossy, but matte gelatin printing-out papers were produced in small numbers before 1900. The image colors of gelatin printing-out papers were typical of gold-toned photolytic silver images, and ranged from reddish-brown to purplish-brown or purple. Under the microscope, the image has continuous tone and the thick, smooth baryta coating totally obscures the fibers of the support. Characteristic forms of deterioration include all of the normal manifestations of photolytic silver image deterioration (highlight detail loss, color shift to yellow-brown, and overall fading), plus a higher incidence of sulfiding deterioration from residual thiosulfates than occurs in albumen prints. Gelatin printing-out paper was extensively used for commercial portraiture during the 1890s, usually in the cabinet-card format. Amateur photographers also used the material in large amounts, generally in the 4 x 5-inch size, to make contact prints from 4 x 5-inch dry-plate negatives. This print material is very difficult to distinguish from glossy collodion printing-out paper using only visual and microscopic examination.

GLOSSY COLLODION PRINTING-OUT PAPERS

Used late 1880s to 1920s. Their surface is very smooth and glossy, especially when mounted and burnished in a heated roller device. The range of image colors is typical of gold-toned printing-out papers, extending from reddish-brown through purplish-brown to purple. Under microscopic examination, the image has continuous tone, and all trace of the paper fibers of the support is obscured by a smooth baryta coating. Characteristic forms of deterioration include overall fading, highlight detail loss, changes in image hue, and abrasion of the collodion binder layer. Like gelatin printing-out papers, glossy collodion printing-out paper was also extensively used for commercial portraiture during the 1890s, usually in the cabinet-card format. This material is very difficult to distinguish from glossy gelatin printing-out paper using only visual and microscopic examination.

LETTERPRESS HALFTONES

Made by a photomechanical reproduction process in use from the 1880s to the present day. Letterpress halftones could be printed on any kind of paper stock in any color ink. The process is characterized by a dot pattern which breaks the image into small round circles of ink in light areas. The pattern appears as a checkerboard in the middletones and leaves only small unprinted circles in the deepest shadows. In 19th-century examples,

the dot size is rather coarse; the halftone screen pattern can usually be seen with the naked eye. Another consequence of the large dot size is poor reproduction of detail. Letterpress halftones will not display image fading.

Letterpress halftones were printed from a relief plate which created a slight indentation wherever ink was deposited. Careful microscopic examination of examples on smooth stock will show that individual dots have crisply defined edges and are outlined with a ridge of ink caused by pressure applied during printing.

MATTE COLLODION PRINTING-OUT PAPERS

Used 1894 to 1920s. Their surface is semi-matte, and their image color is usually neutral or greenish-black as a result of gold-and-platinum toning. This kind of toning imparted excellent image stability so that little or no image fading is observable. Under microscopic examination, the fibers of the paper support are partially visible, and the image has continuous tone. Surface abrasion is a characteristic form of deterioration. The process was extensively used for commercial portraiture from 1895 to 1910. The typical presentation was in the cabinet-card format during the 1890s and on gray, square or rectangular mounts of various sizes after the turn of the 20th century.

PHOTOGRAVURES

Made by a photomechanical reproduction process used from the late 1870s to the present day. Photogravures have a matte surface and may be of any image color. The process was capable of excellent reproduction of detail. Under microscopic examination, the image will have several distinguishing characteristics related to the way ink is deposited on the support. The ink deposit has a speckled appearance and will be broken into a fine, irregular pattern known as an aquatint grain. It is best observed in a textured highlight area. Some photogravures will have an aquatint grain, while others will have a regular screen pattern seen in middletone areas as a square grid of white lines on a dark field. The screen pattern is very fine and individual dots have soft, ragged edges. Less ink is deposited in the lighter image areas than in the shadow areas.

Photogravures will show no signs of image fading. A plate mark (an embossed rectangular outline in the support) may be present, but may have been trimmed off. Mechanical damage and the common forms of paper deterioration (discoloration, embrittlement, and foxing) may be present. Photogravures were used extensively for book illustration and for publishing topographic views.

PLATINOTYPES

Used 1880 to 1930s. Platinotypes (also known as platinum prints) have a matte surface and a black or slightly bluish-black image color; a few have a warmer, brownish hue. Platinotypes have excellent image stability, and no overall fading or localized image deterioration will be found. Upon microscopic examination, the image shows a continuous progression of tones and appears to reside in the paper fibers as a stain rather than a surface deposit. The fibers of the paper support are clearly visible, and the microscopic appearance of a platinotype surface is identical to that of an uncoated book page.

Characteristic forms of deterioration are discoloration and embrittlement of the primary support. A positive "transfer image" may be present on a folder, wrapper, or paper sleeve which has been in contact with the image side of the print during storage. Platinotypes were widely used for commercial portraiture only after the turn of the 20th century.

SALTED PAPERS

Used 1840 to mid-1860s. Surface is matte, and various weights of paper were used. Image colors range from red-brown (untoned) to purple (gold-toned). Microscopic examination shows surface to be identical to an uncoated book page. The image has continuous tone and appears to reside in, rather than on, the paper fibers. The first salted paper prints preceded any kind of stylized mounts, so forms of presentation can vary. Signs of image deterioration typical of photolytic silver are usually present. The most common are edge fading, loss of highlight detail, and a hue shift toward yellow-brown. Though its initial use in the 1840s and 1850s was largely for landscapes and topographical views, the process was revived and used to some extent by fine art and even some professional photographers from 1890 to 1910.

WOODBURYTYPES

Used 1866 to about 1900. The surface of woodburytypes usually shows a definite relief effect, most noticeable at boundaries between very light and very dark image areas. The image may be of any color, but is usually a purple-brown shade chosen to approximate an albumen print. No image fading will be present. Although photomechanical in origin, under microscopic examination, the image has continuous tone, and various-sized specks of undispersed pigment may be present. Red, black, and blue specks can sometimes be distinguished, indicating that a particular color was achieved by blending pigments. Paper fibers will be visible in highlight areas of woodburytypes, but are likely to be obscured by heavy deposits of pigmented gelatin in the darkest shadow areas.

Woodburytypes and carbon prints may be impossible to distinguish from each other using only visual and microscopic examination. Prints larger than 11 x 14-inches (28.6 x 36.2 cm) are unlikely to be woodburytypes. A characteristic form of deterioration of woodburytypes is cracking of the pigmented gelatin binder layer. It is often most severe in high-density areas where the gelatin binder is thickest. Woodburytypes were mainly used for book illustration and large-edition publishing of portraits and topographical views. They were typically trimmed flush and adhered to book pages rather than printed on the same sheet with type matter.

Chapter V:

PRESERVATION AND COLLECTION MANAGEMENT

The essential goal in managing a photographic collection must always be to use photographs in ways that do not contribute to their destruction. The management of a collection of 19th-century photographic prints requires planning, organization and an awareness of the special needs of the prints.

In order to be successful, preservation efforts need to be integrated into every aspect of the storage and use of a collection. The effects of collection policies and practices on the physical well-being of photographs must be carefully anticipated and closely monitored once the policies are in practice.

This chapter tells how preservation relates to the ways in which photographs are collected and used. This information applies to collections of all sizes. The complexity of management problems such as cataloging obviously grows with the size of a collection. But it is just as important to establish order in a small collection as in a large one, and even a small family collection can benefit from a review of the issues discussed here.

This chapter is not intended to be a complete manual for organizing and managing a photographic collection. Cataloging schemes, user policies, security, and other issues pertinent to a comprehensive management program are too complex and specialized to fall within the scope of this book. Collection management functions will only be considered here insofar as they affect preservation.

DEFINING THE PURPOSE AND SIGNIFICANCE OF A COLLECTION

Preservation is not an end in itself. It becomes important only when applied to an artifact which has been judged to be of permanent value. Much of this book describes the sensitivity of 19th-century photographic prints to their environment and the ease with which prints can be damaged by careless handling. The pres-

ervation of such fragile objects requires active effort, may involve considerable expense, and usually restricts the ways in which they can be used. The effort and resources needed to care for 19th-century prints should not (and most likely will not) be expended until the value and purposes of the collection in which they are contained have been clearly defined.

All collections, large or small, should have written statements defining their reasons for existence and generally describing their acquisition and user policies.[42] Most collections that are part of a larger institution contribute to the broad goals set forth in that institution's *mission statement.* In any case, every collection should have its own collection policy explaining how the collection's specific mission will be fulfilled and defining what kinds of objects are to be collected. The *collection policy* should also define the purpose and significance of the collection and establish who may use it.

A collection policy should ideally be completed while a collection is being planned and before any material is acquired. Most collections, however, grow with only a loosely defined purpose, making it more difficult to assign preservation priorities and increasing the risk that the most important materials will not get the attention they deserve.

Deterioration in photographs is often imperceptibly slow. It is not obvious from day to day, for example, how environmental factors or poor storage enclosures affect prints. This subtle pace of deterioration tends to obscure the long-term importance of coordinated preservation policies and can foster a stubborn inertia about initiating such policies.

When a collection's purposes and significance have never been, or have only loosely been formulated, the preparation of a thorough collection policy can renew preservation efforts. By defining the most significant materials, the policy provides an opportunity to review whether their storage and use are consistent with their preservation. Whatever the purpose and significance of a collection, it is vital that its preservation policies be formulated in view of the collection's stated purposes.

ESTABLISHING ORDER

The preservation of 19th-century photographic prints depends on a high degree of order and organization in all collection activities. To organize a collection it is necessary to know what is in it, where the material is stored, and how it will be used. Careless or unnecessary handling results when a collection does not have an inventory, a cataloging scheme, and a filing and retrieval system that complement the collection's uses. The handling of photographs by staff or users can be kept to a minimum through careful planning and organization.

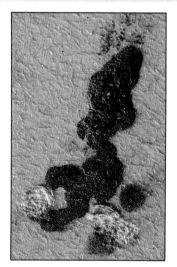

Initial appraisal of collection material should include screening for special preservation problems. This early 1870s albumen print is contaminated by insect debris. A detail of the affected area at 30X magnification is shown below.

James M. Reilly
Photomacrograph,
Caterina Salvi

A high degree of organization and strict inventory procedures are especially important in large collections. Shown here is a portion of the holdings of the Still Pictures Branch, National Archives and Records Administration, Washington, D.C.

National Archives and Records Administration

INVENTORY

An inventory of collection material is essential for preservation and for many other purposes. Regardless of how a collection is arranged or filed, it is necessary to know what photographic processes are represented, and which prints are mounted, unmounted, or in album form. More specifically, a record should exist for each item listing the nature of the object, a physical description of it, and an evaluation of its condition. Each object should have a unique accession number or other identifying code to accompany it through all other record-keeping or cataloging procedures and to verify ownership and

identity. Like a book incorrectly shelved in a library, a photograph not represented in an inventory is effectively lost to a collection.

APPRAISAL AND EVALUATION OF COLLECTION MATERIAL

Evaluating collection materials for their content and significance and for any special preservation problems they present is an important function of collection management. Such an evaluation should be systematically performed on all existing collection materials and should be a standard accession procedure so that all incoming materials are appraised before being added to the storage and cataloging systems. This procedure helps funnel preservation resources to the most important collection materials.

Continual screening of the collection for special preservation problems is important, especially for new material. There are two kinds of problems to look for: those involved with the physical structure of the print, such as extreme fragility or existing physical damage, and external problems such as active mold colonies, insect infestation, or other foreign matter that can threaten other objects in the collection.

Albums, scrapbooks, and other print assemblages also present problems. Their physical soundness must be considered as well as the fact that the prints have been assembled into a unit. It is usually desirable to keep albums and other assemblages in their original form, but the preservation aspects of this decision must be carefully weighed.

CATALOGING AND ACCESS

Cataloging and access tools aid preservation by minimizing or eliminating the need to handle original prints. The degree to which this is possible depends on the needs a collection serves and the quality of the collection's "finding-aids" and cataloging system. Many uses for photographs do not require that an original print be seen, so as a broad principle it is important to convey in a catalog entry as much information as can be abstracted from a photograph. This task is made easier if it is specifically known what kind of information most users want.

When access to original prints is important, finding-aids and catalogs should expediently get users to the objects they need without having to (or having the chance to) examine or handle any others. In many cases, a catalog listing that includes a visual record of an object will avoid unnecessary handling of the original. Visual finding-aids can take the form of a small photographic print attached to a catalog card, an 8 x 10-inch copy print, 35 mm microfilm, a microfiche catalog, or even a computer-linked video disk. All such aids are extremely beneficial to preservation.

USER POLICIES

An inherent conflict exists between preservation and use in all photographic collections, but the delicate nature of 19th-century photographic prints makes it especially important that they be handled with caution and respect in accordance with the guidelines provided by a comprehensive user policy. User policies which either ignore preservation needs or completely restrict access to original materials are not in the best interests of a collection. What is needed is a balanced approach based on understanding how collection materials are actually used, preparing materials to withstand physical wear during use, and teaching all staff and patrons how to use materials responsibly.[43]

The collection policy should include guidelines on how materials are to be used. If more than one use is envisioned, the policy should clearly distinguish between primary and secondary functions. Most institutional collections serve more than one purpose: some function as a historical collection, as an image source for publications, and even as a fine art collection all at the same time. Each of the functions makes different organizational and preservation demands. Without a clear definition of the long-term goals and primary function of the collection, the photographs may suffer when used in ways for which they have not been adequately prepared.

MINIMIZING THE HANDLING OF ORIGINAL PRINTS

In a real sense, to use photographs is to use them up. It is always preferable to substitute copy prints for valuable originals in any use or exhibition which does not require the original. The term "copy" refers to a continuous-tone, photographic copy made from a negative. It should be distinguished from a "photocopy" made by an electrostatic process on an office-type copying machine. Very valuable or heavily used items should always be photographically copied because of the greater risk or likelihood of them being damaged during handling. Any collection which regularly serves as a source of reproductions should have an effective system for creating master negatives or transparencies so that originals need not be constantly rephotographed.

RESPONSIBLE USE OF ORIGINAL PRINTS

Much can be done to protect prints in collections that need to provide original material to viewers for examination. All original prints should be housed in some kind of packaging as protection against finger oils, dust, and dirt. Anyone who comes in contact with original material should be educated in proper handling procedures. Perhaps the most efficient way to do this is to provide a written or audiovisual orientation which briefly outlines the significance of the collection, explains its general organization, and describes proper handling. Users should be warned beforehand that future access to the collection will be based on the care and respect they show for photographs. Do not overlook the need also to educate staff members in these procedures because they most frequently handle collection material.

There is an important psychological element in encouraging respect for the fragility of photographs. The protective packaging in which prints and albums are housed, along with a clean, orderly reading room or work area, and the example of slow, careful handling on the part of staff can all combine to impress users with the need to respect the collection. Those who work most closely with the collection should set a good example not only for users, but also for other staff who may handle collection material. It is also prudent to screen users in advance. Allow access to valuable original materials only to those involved in legitimate research, and then only upon prior application. This gives the staff time to find and prepare the material for examination and discourages casual browsing.

The viewing or reading room should be spacious, well lighted (preferably by tungsten or other light sources low in UV radiation), and convenient to storage areas. Collection materials should be moved from storage to reading rooms in carts, and all materials should remain in boxes or other protective packages during transport. A sink should be provided for patrons to wash their hands before using the collection. There should always be enough table space for users to unbox and examine objects, take notes, and replace objects in wrappers or boxes without being cramped.

For both security and preservation reasons, users of institutional collection materials should always be in the presence of a staff person. Some objects may be too delicate or awkward for users to handle alone and unsupervised, and the presence of a staff member encourages users to proceed carefully.

EXHIBITION POLICIES

Every collection should have a general policy regarding the exhibition of original prints. The importance of exhibitions to a collection will depend on the nature and purpose of the collection. Exhibitions broaden the audience and the base of financial support for many institutional collections. They are also vital to the mission of fine art and historical collections because they allow for a comprehensive view and an enriched appreciation of a body of photographic work. But exhibitions pose a series of preservation problems and dangers, and in order to exhibit original 19th-century prints without harming them, there must be an understanding of the dangers involved and a consistent policy on using collection material for exhibits.

The display environment is by definition harsher than the storage environment because it adds the factor of light damage to all of the other environmental influences. The handling involved in selecting, inventorying, matting, and framing—not to mention the subsequent unframing and replacement in storage—is another likely source of damage to prints.

A collection's exhibition policy should state in a general way whether

The print reading room in the Photography Department of the Art Institute of Chicago is spacious, well lighted, and environmentally controlled.

Art Institute of Chicago

the exhibition of original material is desirable or allowable and, if so, under what circumstances. Ideally, the exhibition policy should provide guidelines to help decide whether originals or copy prints will be used in a given exhibition. Such a decision cannot always be a matter of policy; to a certain extent, the nature of individual exhibitions will determine whether original prints are more appropriate than copies, but a collection-wide policy protects the majority of objects from damage due to shortsighted or ill-conceived exhibition programs. The quality of the lighting, framing materials, and environmental conditions in the exhibition space should also be considered in formulating an exhibition policy.

There is an understandable human tendency to display the rarest and most important materials in a collection. The unfortunate consequences of this impulse are to be seen in the many collections of 19th-century photographs in which the most prized objects show unusually great photochemical damage and other abuse.

For one reason or another, none of the major 19th-century print processes can safely tolerate prolonged exhibition. Because a print is expected to survive for at least several generations of viewers, it can be safely displayed for only a fraction of that time. A reasonable response to this limitation is to set a finite quantity of exhibition time for the projected life of a print and to carefully ration out parts of that display time over the life of the print. No original print should be exhibited on a continuing, indefinite basis.

LOAN POLICIES AND TRAVELING EXHIBITIONS

Collections are increasingly being called upon to loan photographs to other institutions for exhibition. A collection-wide policy regarding the loaning of prints and their use in traveling exhibition is an essential element of preservation planning.

A loan policy is an outgrowth of a general exhibition policy. It should provide guidelines as to what collection materials can be loaned, and under what circumstances. Many factors need to be considered in loaning a photograph, including its rarity and importance, the reason for the loan request, and any possible benefits the

loan may bring the home collection in the form of favorable publicity or the chance for reciprocal borrowing. The impact of loans on the physical well-being of prints is an important consideration. Loans add to the normal hazards of exhibition—those of shipping and of rapidly changing and potentially harmful environments.

Like exhibition policy, loan policy should be conservative and should balance immediate demands on the collection with a regard for future viewers. Preparing a general policy on loans and traveling exhibitions can give due weight to the long-range view when considering a loan request. In the absence of a coherent policy, the immediate lure of favorable publicity or a desire to cooperate with other institutions can tend to overpower sound preservation judgments. An important consideration in formulating loan policy is the experience a collection has had with loans, in terms both of benefits to the collection and damage to prints.

Even with the most detailed and thoughtful loan policy, each loan request will have unique features and will have to be considered on its own merits. Once the decision has been made to loan a photograph, measures can be taken to lessen the chances that it will be damaged while on loan. A detailed agreement should specify all of the terms and conditions of the loan and fix liability on the borrower for any damages sustained. Such an agreement can require the borrower to insure the object from the time it leaves the home collection until it is returned. The agreement can further require the borrower to furnish proof of such insurance at the value stipulated by the lender. The agreement should detail restrictions for the care and display of the object—its general storage environment, light levels while on display, and any special needs the print may have.

Shipping, with its attendant physical and environmental shocks, is the most hazardous aspect of lending a print.[44] The most successful loans are usually preceded by elaborate packaging and preparation of a print before it leaves its home collection. Matting the print and sealing it into a secure frame can help protect it from the rigors of shipping and environmental changes. Another key element in readying an object for lending is the preparation of a detailed condition report, so that when the print is returned it can be carefully inspected for new damage.

Traveling exhibitions compound the peril to photographic prints because the dangers of shipping, handling, and unfavorable environments multiply with time spent on the road. All of these factors should be carefully considered when valuable 19th-century photographic prints are requested for a traveling exhibition. Inexpert preparation or handling can lead to disaster, and experience has shown that even with expert (and costly) preparation, the risk of physical damage remains high. It is important, too, to know the organizations and institutions mounting the exhibitions and to make sure that they understand how to properly unpack, handle, exhibit, repack, and ship the photographs.

SECURITY

Security includes all measures taken to protect a photographic collection from theft, vandalism, human negligence, and natural disaster. The impact on preservation of these security measures (or the lack of them) can be considerable.

There is great diversity among the issues lumped together under the topic of security. Some of them, such as fire- and intrusion-alarm systems, are specialized technical subjects requiring expert consultation; others, such as how to mark collection materials, are best decided by collection managers.

THEFT PREVENTION

The artistic, historic, or monetary value of many 19th-century photographic prints can tempt thieves. In recent years, the art market prices for photographs have soared—and many of the most valuable images are of 19th-century origin.

But thefts of photographs from collections are not always motivated by money. Prints are taken for a variety of personal reasons, including sentimental attachment and research interests. Prints stolen for resale are sometimes recovered when they are offered to dealers and collections, but there is little chance that materials stolen for non-monetary reasons will ever be recovered.

Theft prevention and effective preservation measures are complementary in many areas. Highly organized systems for inventory, filing, and retrieval make it easier to keep track of collection materials. Especially in larger collections, attention should be directed to controlling the flow of objects out of storage and among staff members. When prints are removed from the normal storage system or work areas by staff, the chances are greater that a print will be misplaced, stolen, or accidentally damaged. A particular problem arises when, without leaving a written record, curatorial or other staff remove prints for examination in offices or other non-secure areas. Where such staff "borrowing" is permitted, there should be procedures to ensure the prompt return of material. In general, the number of staff permitted for any reason to remove photographs from storage should be kept to a minimum; procedures should be devised to trace objects through all functions outside secure storage.

Theft by collection users can often be prevented by appropriate reading-room and user polices. Depending on the nature of the collection and the number of security problems encountered in the past, a variety of measures can be taken. For maximum security, users can be screened and made to show identification before being admitted to the reading room. All coats, purses, briefcases, and packages should be banned from the reading room and left in lockers or a checkroom. Only pencils and notebooks should be permitted, and notebooks should be inspected upon leaving. No smoking, eating, or drinking should be permitted. The layout of the reading room should allow the staff to have a clear view of all users, and users should never be left alone with collection materials. Each user should have ample table space, and the number of photographs being examined by a user at any one time should be limited.

MARKING PRINTS FOR SECURITY AND INVENTORY CONTROL

The question of whether to mark prints for inventory and security purposes is an important preservation issue. Marking prints with accession numbers or other information is use-

ther problem with ink stamps and all other forms of indelible marking is the tendency for stamps to accumulate. Some prints have passed through several collections and bear so many stamps that there is little empty area left on the mount; in some cases, even the photographer's imprint is obscured.

Embossing is another method of indelible marking that, like perforation, is destructive and should never be employed. A mark embossed into a print causes irreparable damage to the paper fibers and binder layer, especially on albumen prints with binder layers that are already cracked and weak.

ful for inventory and has long been regarded as a deterrent to theft. Every collection should carefully consider the marking of original prints and establish a well-defined policy that reflects a conscious decision on the role of marking as both an inventory tool and a security measure.

In the past, the techniques for ineradicable security marking have included embossing, ink marking with pens or stamps, and even perforation. The value of these practices as a deterrent to theft can be argued, but their potential for defacing a print is indisputable.

There are a number of preservation problems with indelible marking. Perforating prints obviously causes irreparable damage in the form of lost areas of the image. Marking with inks, whether in image areas or only on the mounts or backs of prints, presents several difficulties. Some inks bleed in time, moving from the backs of photographs to stain the image on the front. Modern felt-tip pens are notorious for this behavior. And all inks transfer to unwanted areas when still wet, so great care must be taken in applying them.

Many albums and photographically illustrated books in institutional collections are defaced by carelessly applied ink stamps. In some cases, although the stamping was done on the backs of the photographs, the books and albums were closed before the ink could dry, and the ink transferred to photographs on facing pages. Some inks fade in light, while others cause fading of silver images. A fur-

Some inks even cause fading of silver images. The ink inscription on this gelatin developing-out paper print is now outlined by a faded area (30X magnification below).

James M. Reilly
Photomacrograph,
Caterina Salvi

When formulating a policy on marking, the issues of inventory control on the one hand, and theft deterrence and proof of ownership on the other, should be separately considered. The need for marking of any kind should not be assumed, but should always be carefully examined.

Indelible marking as a security measure is only one possible element in an overall security program. Its value as a deterrent must be weighed against the disadvantages of both intentional and accidental defacement.

There are substantial arguments to be made against the use of indelible marking as a security measure. Individuals who take prints for personal, not monetary, reasons will not be deterred by such marks. To lower the value of a stolen print for resale, the mark must be in the image because a serious thief can overcome marks on the mount or the reverse of a print. Marks on the reverse can be covered by remounting, and those on the face of the mount can be trimmed off. The unfortunate trade-off in security marking is that the "security" provided is directly proportional to the defacement of the print.

Alternatives to indelible marking should be used whenever possible. Supplemental security measures—checkrooms for coats and belongings, notebook inspections, close monitoring of reading rooms, and, when appropriate, the use of copies rather than valuable originals—can all deter theft just as well as marking, and do not deface photographs. Effective non-defacing marking systems may yet be developed, but none of the currently available electronic anti-theft systems are suitable for a collection of 19th-century photographic prints.

Reversible Marking for Inventory Control

In some cases the nature of a collection is such that no marking is needed on original prints, even for inventory. More often, however, a mark to identify each photograph is a necessary feature of an inventory system. Accession numbers, in which each photograph has a unique identifying code number, are the most common type of inventory control marking. In general, the marking of prints for any reason should be kept to the barest minimum; when inventory marking is practiced, the mark should be small, discreet, and, above all, reversible.

Reversible marking is best done with a #2 graphite pencil. A softer pencil tends to smear, while a harder pencil, such as a #3, requires too much pressure to make a legible mark and can emboss a print and damage binder layers. No other writing implements or marking devices should be used. Ballpoint pens, felt-tip pens, or technical pens should never be used on any part of a photograph or its mount. Do not use pressure-sensitive or gummed labels of any kind on either prints or enclosures (including plastic enclosures). Accession numbers should be marked in pencil, generally along a bottom edge of the back of a photograph or its mount. Should the print be subsequently matted or encapsulated, the accession number (along with any other information on the back of the print or mount) should be transferred to the mat or encapsulation board, again using a #2 pencil.

PREVENTING AND RESPONDING TO EMERGENCIES

An important area in which preservation concerns overlap the management of a photographic collection is in preparing for fires, floods, and other man-made or natural calamities that can destroy a collection.[48] Emergencies that threaten from within, like fire, call for carefully reasoned preventive policies. For disasters that threaten from outside, such as floods, the most appropriate action is to analyze the risks and plan an organized response. It is essential that all preservation programs anticipate possible emergencies, analyze their impact on collection materials, and create response procedures.

FIRE PREVENTION

Few calamities present so great a danger to a collection of photographic prints as fire. A photographic archive is highly flammable, and the water used to combat fires can be as devastating to prints as fire itself. A basic step in fire protection is to construct the storage room and all its fixtures of non-combustible materials. Every collection should maintain an ongoing fire prevention effort that includes surveying the premises for cluttered spaces, faulty or overloaded electrical wiring, and other hazards. There should be a strictly enforced no-smoking policy in all storage and use areas. (In addition to posing a fire hazard, smoking generates ash and coats objects with a tarry residue.)

Fire is one of the worst calamities that can befall a photographic collection. Even though it escaped the flames, this albumen print suffered smoke, water, and mold damage.

James M. Reilly

Fire-detection and fire-suppression systems are essential to a collection's preservation. A sophisticated fire-protection system will include sensors for smoke or heat and an automatically-triggered release of a fire-suppressing substance. Sprinkler systems and carbon dioxide-releasing systems are not suitable for the storage areas of photographic prints. Many collections have automatic fire-suppression systems utilizing HALON,* a colorless gas which effectively puts out fires but does not leave a residue or deposit. Expert technical advice is needed on both fire-detection systems and automatic fire-suppression systems.[46]

DISASTER PLANNING

An effort should be made to estimate the likelihood of various natural and man-made calamities, such as floods, burst pipes, tornadoes, hurricanes, earthquakes, utility outages, explosions, volcanoes, and structural collapse. Volcanic activity is obviously a negligible threat to a collection in New York City; but explosions, utility outages, and water-main breaks are not. These events are not pleasant to contemplate, but the best way to mini-

---
*HALON is a trademark of E. I. duPont de Nemours and Co., Inc.

mize the damage they may cause is by advance planning.

Identifying the most significant objects in a collection is the first step in forming a policy to protect them in an emergency. In light of the most likely types of disasters, adjustments can be made in the storage location and fixtures to guard the most important items.

Another element of disaster planning is the creation of an emergency response team. A disaster plan should be written down and made known to all staff, so that each person knows his or her role in responding to an emergency. It is usually best to designate one staff member to coordinate disaster planning and implement the plan. The conservator or preservation officer (if there is one) should help plan for and respond to any crisis which may threaten collection materials.

When 19th-century photographs have suffered smoke, fire, mechanical, and especially water damage, the help of a photographic conservator will immediately be required. Every disaster plan should therefore include arrangements for emergency conservation services. Few collections have the luxury of a photographic conservation specialist on staff, so it is important to determine in advance how emergency help can be obtained from private or institutional conservators or a regional conservation facility.[47]

DISASTER RECOVERY

A well-made disaster plan will include procedures for assessing and recovering from various types of damage to collection materials. Water damage is among the most devastating misfortunes that can befall a photographic collection. Prints which have been wetted need urgent attention. If left under water for too long, they will physically disintegrate; if left to dry unattended, stacks of prints and enclosures will weld into solid masses and mold growth will be prolific. Recent research on disaster recovery procedures at the Public Archives of Canada indicates that freezing (but not freeze-drying) is an acceptable means of stabilizing water-soaked 19th-century photographic prints until the attempt to salvage them can be made by a photographic conservation specialist.[48]

Chapter VI:

STORAGE

Storage conditions and storage materials are at the heart of all efforts to preserve 19th-century photographic prints. In contrast to the sudden traumas that occur when a print is damaged during handling or use, the forces threatening a photograph in storage work slowly, often too slowly to attract notice. Moisture, air pollution, and heat in the storage environment can set in motion the chemical processes of deterioration; these factors can further damage prints by allowing molds, bacteria, and insects to flourish.

Prints in storage need the fullest possible protection against excess pressure, dust, abrasion, and other causes of mechanical damage. They even need protection from each other, because such things as flaking bronze inks or highly lignified mounts can damage neighboring prints in a storage container. Storage conditions and the quality of housing materials affect *all* of the photographs in a collection *all* the time—and most forms of deterioration associated with poor storage are irreversible. That is why providing proper storage is so important, and why upgrading storage conditions and materials is one of the most positive steps that can be taken to preserve a collection of 19th-century photographic prints.

THE STORAGE ENVIRONMENT

Of the many types of photographs found in collections, 19th-century prints are among the most sensitive to environmental conditions. (The reasons for this are detailed in Chapters II and III, which discuss the mechanisms of deterioration for the components of prints and for each of the specific print types.)

There is a distinct hierarchy of damaging effects that an inadequate storage environment can cause in prints. First, the most harmful of these effects is the oxidation of silver images, which leads both to the loss of pictorial information through fading

and to changes in image color. The next major category of damage is the chemical and biological deterioration of binders, supports and all kinds of secondary supports, including albums. For example, the discoloration of paper, embrittlement, the yellowing of albumen, and the potential for poor quality papers to stain neighboring objects are all related to the nature of the storage environment. The third most severe effect is physical damage from the changes in size and shape due to variations in the moisture content of prints and their mounts.

In order to provide adequate storage for photographs, it is necessary to understand both the workings of the environment and the role of environmental factors in deterioration. Our view of the environment is largely derived from what we are able to sense directly—that is, from the feelings of comfort or discomfort the environment produces in us. But we are poorly equipped to sense the many subtle environmental agents that can damage a photograph. For example, only at extremes of dryness and dampness are we aware of the relative humidity of the air, yet photographs can be seriously affected long

---

ENVIRONMENTAL FACTORS IN THE DETERIORATION OF 19TH-CENTURY PHOTOGRAPHIC PRINTS

1. Relative Humidity

   Low: 0—30% RH
   Moderate: 30—50% RH
   High: 50—70% RH
   Very High: 70—100% RH

2. Temperature

3. Air Pollution

   —Particulates
   —Oxidant Gases
   —Acidic Gases
   —Sulfiding Gases

before a humidity shift is perceptible to our senses. Only in the most extreme cases will pollutants in indoor air become detectable to us because of their odor or the irritation they cause, although they can damage prints at much lower levels.[49] To prolong the life of photographs, it is necessary to use special equipment to measure and control the environmental factors that affect them.

RELATIVE HUMIDITY

Relative humidity (RH) is undoubtedly the single most important environmental agent and the key to the preservation (or destruction) of 19th-century photographic prints. RH is a measure of how saturated the air is with moisture. The degree of saturation is important because it controls how much moisture will be gained or lost by all water-absorbing materials. At room temperature (20°C) and half-saturation of the air (50% RH), paper contains about 5% water by weight, and albumen 15%. Raising the RH to 80% nearly doubles the water content of both materials, so that paper contains 8-9% water, and albumen about 30%. Regardless of temperature, it is the relative humidity of the surrounding air which determines the moisture content of water-absorbing objects like photographic prints.

The Effects of Low RH

Relative humidity expresses the degree of saturation of the air as a percentage (that is, as a number from 0 to 100, with the air holding all the moisture it can at 100% RH). In considering the preservation needs of photographs, the range of possible humidities can be subdivided into three regions: low (0-30%), moderate (30-50%), and high (50-100%). At low humidities, all of the chemical deterioration processes which require water (most notably the oxidation of silver images) are either completely stopped or slowed to a minimum, and biological deterioration from mold growth is virtually eliminated. In spite of these advantages, the low RH region is unsuitable for storing photographs because it makes paper, albumen, and gelatin so brittle that they can easily be damaged during handling. Low humidity can also cause serious physical damage due to uneven shrinkage among the various components of a print.

Ideal Storage: The Moderate RH Region

The moderate (30-50%) RH region is most desirable for the storage of 19th-century photographic prints. It is dry enough to inhibit chemical or biological deterioration, and moist enough to keep cellulosic materials and proteins flexible. Objects can be handled safely, and they deteriorate much more slowly than at higher humidities. When mechanical control systems and the needs of other objects permit, the storage environment for 19th-century photographic prints should be within the lower half of the moderate humidity range, between 30-40% RH.

It is important to note that the ideal humidity range for photographs is not always best for other types of objects. Some leathers, for example, may be too brittle to be safely handled below 40% RH. For some wooden objects, especially panel paintings and musical instruments, 30% RH may be too dry. Although photographic prints have paper supports, the recommended RH range for the storage of photographs is slightly lower than that for paper documents. This reflects the overwhelming importance of inhibiting the oxidation of silver images. Paper documents are usually best stored between 40 and 50% RH.[50] The inks and pigments found in books, documents and artworks on paper are not as moisture-sensitive as the photolytic silver images in 19th-century photographic prints. Therefore, the recommended humidity range for paper and books is higher, and because of additional flexibility due to a higher moisture content, the

The print storage vault at the Art Institute of Chicago operates at 15°C (60°F), 40% RH all year round. It provides an ideal environment for the storage of photographic prints.

Art Institute of Chicago

danger of damage during handling is somewhat reduced. On the other hand, the relative dryness recommended for photographs makes it important to use extra care in handling leather objects, such as albums, or items already embrittled by deterioration.

The Effects of High RH

There is a rapidly escalating level of damage to prints exposed to the high (50-100%) RH region. Between 50 and 60% RH, there is a gradual increase in the moisture content of albumen and gelatin, but the situation is not yet devastating. Above 60%, there is a very rapid increase in moisture content and the threat of image oxidation (fading) becomes very serious. At levels between 65 and 70%, the spread of fungus becomes possible. Each small rise in humidity above 70% RH is more destructive than the last.

The accompanying graph shows the relationship between the moisture content of albumen and the extent of image fading. The upper curve on the graph represents the amount (by weight) of water in albumen at different relative humidities.[51] The lower curve represents the degree of image fading (density loss) observed in the shadow areas of albumen prints during accelerated aging tests carried out at various RH levels.[20]

The similarity of the two curves—particularly their steepness above 65% RH—shows the close relationship between moisture content and image deterioration. Although the fading data in the graph were obtained from accelerated tests, they accurately represent the long-term effect of relative humidity on albumen prints in storage.

Accelerated aging tests on albumen prints reveal some additional facts about the relationship between RH and image deterioration. Even at room temperature, serious fading occurs within days when albumen prints are exposed to high humidities. A short period of high humidity can cause damage which would take much, much longer at a moderate RH. All oxidative image attack is cumulative—once fading occurs, the damage cannot be reversed. Moreover, the extent of cumulative deterioration in collections of 19th-century photo-

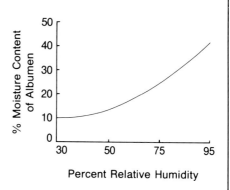

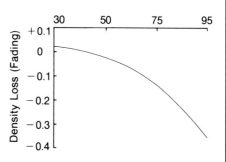

Relationship of Relative Humidity to Image Fading of Albumen Prints

graphs correlates in a rough way with the average outdoor RH of a particular locality. Collections of albumen prints which have long resided in naturally dry areas are generally in much better condition than those in collections located in humid areas. Image deterioration of the sulfiding type due to residual processing chemicals or atmospheric sulfur is also more rapid at high RH.

There is more than image attack to fear from high RH. The yellowing of albumen is also dependent on the moisture content of the albumen layer.[31] Other chemical forms of deterioration activated by high RH include the fading of dyes and the entire set of problems related to poor quality paper. Mounts and mats containing lignin degrade at a rate dependent on RH and release peroxides that fade silver images. The degradation products of lignin are acidic and cause "wood-burn" stains. Not only does lignin degrade faster at higher RH, but the migration of harmful substances is greatly aided by high moisture content.

In short, the relative humidity of the storage environment functions as a kind of speed control for many of the chemical processes that cause deterioration. Slowing down deteriorative processes is largely a matter of keeping relative humidity at recommended levels.

Biological Deterioration at High RH

A companion problem to image fading at sustained high relative humidity is the growth of fungi. Though the spores of these microscopic plants are found nearly everywhere in the environment, they will not germinate and grow at relative humidities less than about 65%.[52] They flourish at sustained high RH, particularly where ventilation is lacking. Though molds can grow on almost anything, photographic prints are an ideal food source for them. Again, the best prevention is RH control. Prints and albums damaged by mold should be isolated to prevent their millions of spores from contaminating the main storage areas. All attempts to clean or restore seriously mold-damaged prints should be left to a professional conservator.

Bacteria can also be a factor in the deterioration of photographic prints, but they only grow when RH remains very high for extended periods.

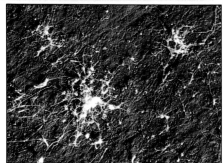

The arrow points to the location of a mold colony on a gelatin developing-out paper print. The affected area is shown magnified 30X at right.

Constance McCabe
Photomacrograph,
Caterina Salvi

EFFECTS OF HIGH RH ON 19TH-CENTURY PHOTOGRAPHIC PRINTS

1. Chemical
   —Oxidation of Silver Images (Fading)
   —Deterioration of Supports
   —Yellowing of Albumen

2. Biological
   —Growth of Fungi
   —Growth of Bacteria
   —Greater Insect Damage

3. Physical
   —Sticking of Gelatin to Enclosures
   —Changes in Size and Shape

Many types of insects which can harm photographs likewise flourish at high RH levels though lower humidities do not effectively eliminate them.

The Effects of RH on Size and Shape

For water-absorbing materials like paper, gelatin, and albumen, the changes in size and shape caused by variations in moisture content are much greater than expansions or contractions due to temperature. As its moisture content rises, machine-made paper expands with a highly directional character, increasing in length mostly along the axis perpendicular to the machine direction. Albumen and gelatin tend to expand uniformly in all directions with increasing moisture content, but their total expansion is greater than that of paper. Swollen gelatin in particular is very soft and can easily be damaged or adhere to adjacent materials. Paper that loses moisture under dry conditions shrinks with the same directional character, but albumen and gelatin do not. At the dry extreme, the shrinkage of protein materials is also greater than that of paper.

Most of the time these physical changes are reversible and do not greatly harm individual components that can freely respond to changes in ambient relative humidity. Of course, in photographic prints the components are laminated and cannot freely expand and contract. At the extremes of RH, the differential rates of expansion and contraction lead to binder cracking, delamination, tears, and irreversible warpage. Since the absorption or loss of water by all components may not occur at the same rate, fast cycling of RH (even within limits considered safe under stable conditions) can be very damaging.

Measuring and Controlling Relative Humidity

In light of its importance in the storage conditions for 19th-century photographic prints, it is essential to understand the nature of relative humidity and how to measure and control it.

We have seen that *regardless of temperature*, RH determines whether photographs gain or lose moisture. But it is equally important to note that temperature strongly influences the RH of a closed system, such as the air in a room or building. The temperature determines how much water air can hold; warm air can hold much more water than cold air. The amount of water in the air, expressed as so many grams of water per cubic meter, is called the *absolute humidity*, as opposed to *relative humidity*, the measure of water saturation in the air. The formula for computing relative humidity is as follows:

$$\%RH = \frac{\text{amount of water in a quantity of air}}{\text{amount of water the air can hold at that temperature.}} \times 100$$

Saturation, or 100% RH, occurs when the air is holding all the water it can. When the air is holding only half the water it can, the RH is 50%. But because temperature determines the amount of water that air can hold (the denominator on the RH formula), a rise in temperature will lower the RH of air in a closed system. Conversely, cooling the air will drive up the relative humidity. For example, one reason why basements are damp is because they are cool. Air from other parts of a structure may be at 21°C (70°F) and 50% RH, but when cooled to 13°C (55°F) in the basement, the RH will rise to 85%.

RH Measurement

A way to measure RH is needed if humidity is to be monitored and controlled in the storage environment. For several reasons, it is not practical to determine how much water a given volume of air contains and directly compute the RH using the formula above. It is more efficient to determine RH indirectly by measuring changes in the size or shape of a water-absorbing material. The best of the instruments designed to do this is the *hair hygrometer*, the mechanism of which is based on the fact that the length of a strand of human hair varies directly with relative humidity. The expansion and contraction of a hair in the device causes a pivot to move a dial pointer (or, in a recording-type instrument, a pen). Hair hygrometers are familiar sights in museums and archives, usually in the form of recording hygro-thermographs, which create a continuous record of temperature and humidity on a chart wrapped around a clockwork-driven drum. All hair hygrometers must be initially calibrated and periodically rechecked to ensure the accuracy of their readings. Less expensive hygrometers that use paper or other materials to sense RH are not as accurate as hair hygrometers.

Another, more intrinsically accurate type of RH-measuring instrument is the *wet-and-dry-bulb psychrometer*, which is based on the cooling effect of evaporation. Two thermometers are used: one is a standard "dry-bulb" thermometer; and the other is identical except that its reservoir bulb of mercury is covered with a moistened wick, a snug-fitting sleeve of cotton kept moist with distilled water. For the instrument to work, air must be moved past the thermometer at a fairly rapid rate. This can be done by fanning the thermometers, or, as with the *sling psychrometer*, by whirling both thermometers around a pivot.

As air moves past the wick of the wet-bulb thermometer, the water in the wick evaporates. Heat is consumed when water is converted from liquid to vapor, so the wick cools off and the reading on the wet-bulb thermometer decreases. The more evaporation that takes place, the greater the cooling. The extent of cooling, called the "wet-bulb depression," has a direct relationship to RH. If the air is already saturated with water, no evaporation and hence no cooling will take place; the lower the RH, the larger the wet-bulb depression. After a few moments of fanning or whirling, an equilibrium is reached and the temperature of the wet-bulb thermometer remains steady. At this point, the RH may be determined by using charts which relate the three quantities of dry-bulb temperature, wet-bulb temperature, and RH. Such charts are usually built into sling psychrometers in the form of a "slide-rule" scale.

Wet-and-dry-bulb instruments are reliable enough to use for checking and calibrating hair and paper hygrometers, but need to be used carefully to attain the true minimum wet-bulb temperature. If the wet-bulb temperature is too high, the RH determination will also be too high. The reading on the wet-bulb thermometer should be taken as soon as the fanning or whirling is stopped. Make several readings to ensure that the true minimum is obtained. False readings can also occur if the wick is dirty or contaminated with residues from tap water. For maximum accuracy in wet-and-dry-bulb RH determinations, the thermometers should exactly agree when tested with a dry wick and no fanning.

In addition, there are electronic RH-measuring devices that monitor changes of conductivity, resistance, or capacitance due to varying moisture levels. Electronic instruments offer convenience and speed of measurement, and they are very useful in monitoring and in control systems for climate-controlled spaces. They are costly, however, and need to be checked and calibrated with wet-and-dry-bulb instruments or special calibrating devices.

Automatic Systems for Controlling Relative Humidity in Large Areas

Very few photographic collections are located in climates that naturally remain all year at the ideal 30-40% RH. Temperate zones usually have humidities that are too high in summer and too low in winter.

Localized temperature differences can cause pockets of high or low RH within a building, or even within a room. Begin protecting a collection against high or low humidity by studying RH readings made in the storage area by a reliable instrument. RH problems can then be analyzed and dealt with, either by installing apparatus to control humidity, or by finding a new storage situation for collection materials.

It is very difficult in practice to keep humidity in the ideal 30-40% range, but it remains necessary to make the attempt. Because of the relationship between temperature and RH, full humidity control is usually based on the capacity to heat the air, cool it, add water to it (humidify), or dry it (dehumidify)—each as required. In summer, when the outdoor RH is high and the air is warm, cooling and dehumidification are necessary; in winter, when the outdoor air is cold, heating and humidification are required. All four actions may be needed during transitional periods.

The mechanical apparatus for automatically sensing and controlling temperatures and RH is expensive and bulky, and rarely works as well as hoped. The most consistent, trouble-free operation is provided by new installations in which the entire storage area is designed and constructed as a controlled environment. The position of the storage area within a structure, air-flow patterns, duct arrangement, and the location of the mechanical apparatus can then all be optimized. These systems require careful planning. Most of their problems arise not from technical difficulties, but from a lack of communication between collection managers, architects, engineers, and contractors. It is much more difficult to install a humidity control system in an existing structure, and the costs are accordingly much higher.

Room Humidifiers and Dehumidifiers

Small, portable equipment may be helpful when a collection lacks general humidity-control systems and RH records indicate problems with high RH, low RH, or cycling. Separate equipment is needed for humidifying and for dehumidifying. These units cannot provide the constant RH control that is ideal for storing 19th-century prints, but they can perform a valuable service by alleviating extremes of dryness or dampness.

Most portable dehumidifiers are of the refrigerant type, in which room air is blown by a fan over cooling coils. As the air is cooled, its RH rises to 100% and water begins to condense on the coils. The condensed water drips into a pan and is collected or, preferably, drained away. The refrigeration system of a dehumidifier also has a set of coils which are warm. The air, after giving up much of its moisture during the cooling process, passes over the warm coils and is dried and slightly heated. Refrigerant dehumidifiers are generally best for temporary or emergency installation in a photographic storage area. They cannot over-dry the air, and their only potential hazard is spillage of the water they collect.

When temporary or emergency humidification is needed, the best equipment to use is an unheated evaporative humidifier. This consists of a fan, a porous pad which rotates in front of the fan, and a reservoir of water. As the pad turns it is dipped into the water, and then passes through the current of air created by the fan. This evaporates the water and slightly cools the pad and the air.

Problems with evaporative humidifiers include algae and slime growth in the water reservoir and the build-up of scale on the evaporative pad. It is important to keep the water reservoir clean because some bacteria can act on the algal slime to release hydrogen sulfide. Demineralized water should be used because tap water may form a mineral scale that can clog the evaporative pad.

All portable humidifiers and dehumidifiers have inherent limitations. They have a limited capacity, and cannot compensate for building ventilation systems that pour too much dry or damp air into storage areas. Likewise, they may not be able to overcome situations in which moisture gain or loss through walls is too great, as in a very damp basement. Poor air mixing may keep the RH changes produced by small units from extending throughout a storage area. It is always necessary to check the RH conditions immediately surrounding photographs.

TEMPERATURE

Heat is a form of energy which increases the rate of nearly all chemical reactions, including those that cause the deterioration of 19th-century photographs. The storage temperature for photographic prints should therefore be kept as low as it can while being consistent with the practical considerations of limiting the cost of temperature control and allowing access to the collection. High temperatures imperil photographs, but high RH can cause far greater damage. The combination of high temperature and high RH is one of the worst environmental calamities that can befall a collection.

It is desirable to maintain a low temperature in the storage area, and most kinds of photographic prints are not harmed even by very low temperatures. But practical difficulties arise, especially when storage temperatures get much below 15°C (60°F). Cooling the air increases its relative humidity, so that ever greater dehumidification capacity is needed as the storage area becomes cooler. Below 18°C (65°F) people can no longer work comfortably in the storage area for extended periods. Depending on conditions in adjacent areas, there may be a danger of condensation when objects are brought from cool storage into warmer rooms.

Thus, without a specially constructed vault, it is difficult to achieve safe low-temperature storage conditions. In the future, when more is known about the mechanisms of deterioration, low-temperature storage may be considered a necessary preservation measure for unstable materials like albumen prints. At present, the recommended storage temperature for all 19th-century photographic prints is 18°C (65°F) or below. Daily fluctuations in temperature greater than about 4°C (7°F) should be avoided.

AIR POLLUTION

The third significant factor in the storage environment for 19th-century photographic prints is air pollution. The majority of the dangerous forms of pollution originate from the burning of fuels: gasoline in automobiles, and coal and oil in heating plants and power plants. The level of pollutants indoors is generally lower than outdoors, unless the pollutant is generated within a building, room, or even a storage box. The most potent threats to photographs come from solid forms of air pollution, called particulates, and from gaseous pollutants of the oxidant and sulfiding type.

Particulates

Particulates are solids suspended in the air. Their size can vary over a wide range, but the largest particulates tend to settle close to their source. Combustion causes soot and smoke, which form a large portion of the solids in the atmosphere. These hydrocarbons and ash particles are greasy and dirty; they may have acidic gases adsorbed to them. Other kinds of particulates come from mechanical processes such as sawing and grinding, and from natural sources, such as pollen, silicate particles, and salt spray. The indoor environment is polluted with textile fibers and bits of skin and hair, as well as many particulates which infiltrate from the outdoors. Particulates in the indoor environment collectively cause dust, which is grimy, abrasive, and can be chemically or biologically active.

The best defense against particulates is a two-tiered approach of providing air filtration for the entire storage area and individual dust protection for all objects. The only way to remove particulates from a storage area is to install filters in the air-handling system. Typically, several filters are installed in sequence to trap various sizes of particles. Air from the outdoors should be filtered before entering the system, and recirculated air should be filtered as well. In spite of any filtration system which may be in place, all objects should be housed in containers to protect them from dust. Such protection is also important for other reasons, but avoiding the accumulation of dust on photographs is easy to do and essential to their preservation.

A note of caution: electrostatic air purifiers are very effective at removing particulates from the air, but should not be used in photographic storage areas because they generate ozone, an oxidant gas which can cause fading of silver images.

Oxidant Gases

Oxidant gases are a form of air pollution particularly threatening to photographs.[27] Oxidant pollution is a byproduct of modern urban life, and while the levels of particulates have been falling in recent years, the levels of oxidant gases in the atmosphere have been rising. There are two important oxidant gases: nitrogen dioxide and ozone. Nitrogen dioxide is largely created by the running of automobile engines and other combustion processes. Ozone occurs naturally but can also be formed when light acts on the nitrogen oxides produced by automobile exhausts. Heavy electrical machinery can create high levels of ozone, as can some types of lamps used in electrostatic copy machines.

The sources of oxidant gases in the storage environment for photographs are not necessarily outside the box, storage room, or building. Apart from the major atmospheric oxidant gases mentioned above, many other

---

POTENTIAL SOURCES OF OXIDANT GASES

1. Fumes from Curing of Oil-Base Paints
2. Electrostatic Copiers
3. Wood and Wood Finishes
4. Cosmetics and Cleaning Supplies

---

kinds can be generated by substances or processes much closer to the photographs. Organic peroxides from untreated wood or poor quality paper products cause the oxidation of silver images and cellulose, while hydrogen peroxides are produced during the curing of oil-base paints. Cosmetics, cleaning supplies, and some types of newly-manufactured plastics can also pollute the storage environment with oxidant vapors.

The effects of oxidant gases on photographic collections are to be seen in the form of faded images, discolored and embrittled paper, and weakened binder layers. It is always difficult to determine the precise oxidants responsible for deterioration because even minute quantities can cause damage.[53] There should be a three-tiered approach in protecting a collection against oxidant gases: air purification to remove oxidants from the storage atmosphere, vigilance in finding and removing local sources of oxidant pollution, and relative humidity control. The relationship between moisture and the oxidative fading of silver images has been discussed in Chapter II. The same general relationship between moisture and oxidative processes for silver holds for other forms of oxidative deterioration.

Acidic and Sulfiding Gases

The burning of fuels releases products into the atmosphere which react with oxygen and water to form strong acids. Sulfur is present in oil and coal; after combustion, it is discharged into the air as sulfur dioxide. The reaction of sulfur dioxide with oxygen and water ultimately leads to the formation of sulfuric acid. This is the sequence of events responsible for "acid rain." A similar effect causes nitrogen dioxide to form nitric acid, but the sulfur dioxide problem is on a much larger scale. Sulfur dioxide does not directly attack the silver image of photographs, but the absorption of acidic gases tends to promote oxidative image fading and contributes to the embrittlement and discoloration of paper.

Some of the sulfur in fuels ends up as hydrogen sulfide, a virulent pollutant for photographic storage. Hydrogen sulfide is a gas which directly reacts with silver to form silver sulfide. It causes tarnish on daguerreotypes and other bulk silver objects, but is equally threatening to 19th-century silver prints, especially in combination with high relative humidity. Traces of hydrogen sulfide are almost universally present because it has many natural as well as artificial sources. High concentrations of hydrogen sulfide occur in furnace rooms and in photographic darkrooms when "sepia" (controlled sulfiding) toners are used. Certain industrial processes, including some types of paper manufacturing, produce locally high concentrations of hydrogen sulfide.

OVERALL CONTROL OF THE STORAGE ENVIRONMENT

Climatic conditions and atmospheric pollutants vary from region to region and may be affected by very localized geographical features. There may even be special environmental circumstances within a structure or room. The problems involved in minimizing deterioration from environmental causes will therefore always be unique and challenging.

The first step in establishing environmental control is to become aware of the actual conditions prevailing at the storage site. The measurement and record-keeping of storage-room temperatures and RH are fundamental.[54] Beyond that, much useful information about climatic conditions and pollution levels is available from local meteorological services. The variety of substances which can potentially be present makes it difficult to identify specific contaminants in the storage atmosphere; but once a high level of a specific substance is suspected, detection methods can be employed to verify its presence.

Regardless of the specific environmental problems facing a collection, the most successful attempts to limit deterioration from all environmental causes are based on the creation of a storage space with temperature and humidity control, coupled with filtration for particulates and purification equipment to remove oxidant, acidic, and sulfiding gases. Such an integrated approach to environmental control is initially costly, but in the long term is the most efficient way to meet the storage needs of 19th-century photographic prints.

STORAGE MATERIALS

INTERACTION OF STORAGE MATERIALS WITH THE ENVIRONMENT

The primary goal of proper storage for 19th-century photographic prints is to minimize their deterioration. There are two basic elements in the storage system: the environment and the enclosure materials (sleeves, boxes, shelves, and cabinets) which house the prints. The importance of the *interactions* between the housing materials and the environment should not be forgotten during the following discussion of storage materials.

Where environmental conditions are less than optimal, the quality of storage materials becomes much more significant. The release of oxidants, sulfur, peroxides, and acids from poor quality papers and plastics is closely dependent on the environmental factors of RH and temperature. Even where enclosure materials are of the very highest quality, environmental problems can be made worse by, for example, encapsulating prints under conditions of high relative humidity, thereby inadvertently trapping moisture inside the enclosure.

ENCLOSURES AND PROTECTIVE PACKAGING

A key concept in the storage of photographic prints is that each photograph should have its own protective housing.[55] An individual enclosure shields a print from scratches, finger oils, dust, and to a certain degree, the environment. It restrains curl and protects a print from interactions with neighboring prints in storage. An enclosure prepares a print for handling, and has the psychological effect of underscoring the value of the print to potential handlers.

"Loose" prints are quickly battered in handling and use, and no print should remain unprotected. Beyond protecting against such abuse, enclosures have a further purpose within the larger preservation strategy. They are the innermost level of physical protection—a coat of mail, but not the full suit of armor. After being put into individual enclosures, prints should be boxed, and the boxes shelved in metal cabinets. There may be two levels of boxes, or perhaps dividers within a box, to keep the prints from shifting. Albums and other assemblages of photographs also require protective packaging.

"Armoring" the collection and providing multiple layers of packaging are the basis of an approach to storage which gives a high level of physical protection, yet favorably affects the ways in which a collection is used. Multiple levels of packaging slow users down and encourage a sense of order. The point is not to obstruct users frivolously or to create functionless packaging. Each level serves a separate but important purpose.

QUALITY OF ENCLOSURE MATERIALS

Enclosure materials are constructed of either paper or plastic. In both papers and plastics, there are great differences between acceptable, high quality grades and lesser quality products. Because enclosures are so intimately associated with the photographs they hold, it is essential that they be chemically inert and have no undesirable physical properties.

All enclosure materials selected for a collection should conform to the requirements of American National Standards Institute (ANSI) Standard PH 1.53-1984, *Processed Films, Plates, and Papers—Filing Enclosures and Containers for Storage.* Not all products marketed as "archival" or "acid-free" meet the requirements of the ANSI Standard. One of the most important of the Standard's requirements is passage of the "Photographic Activity Test," an accelerated aging test which verifies that an enclosure material does not harm the photographs stored inside it.

ENCLOSURES FOR PHOTOGRAPHIC PRINT PRESERVATION

Each Object Should Have Its Own Enclosure and Packaging to Protect From:

—Dust
—Handling Damage
—Fast Changes in Environmental Conditions

"Armor" the Collection by Providing Multiple Levels of Packaging:

Level 1:—Sleeve, Envelope, or Wrapper
Level 2:—Box or Drawer
Level 3:—Shelf or Cabinet

In such accelerated tests, "archival quality" paper and board products fail more (that is, they more often cause staining and fading of prints) than do the recommended types of plastic materials.[56] There are several reasons for this. Plastics are much more homogeneous materials than paper, and their composition can be carefully controlled. Paper exists in a much wider variety of forms, from thin tissue to multilayer boards. The paper-maker must work with raw materials of varying composition and make extensive use of additives and chemical treatments to obtain a product with the desired weight, color, surface, and physical properties. The chemical complexity of paper makes it difficult to ensure its inertness toward photographs by any means other than testing the finished products. Paper and board products expressly manufactured for inertness toward photographic images have recently appeared on the market. This is a welcome development, and should reduce the uncertainty surrounding paper enclosure materials for photographic storage—*if* the products are actually tested for their effects on photographs.

Choosing Papers and Boards

The safest papers and boards for photographic storage are those which meet the requirements of ANSI Standard PH 1.53-1984. When such products are not available, the following guidelines for selecting papers and boards may be of use. First look for the fiber source used to make the paper or board. Paper consists mostly of cellulose fibers. Wood is a common source of cellulose, but wood contains lignin, waxes, and resins—tenacious non-cellulose impurities which have to be removed by extensive chemical treatment. Cotton and linen are superior to wood as fiber sources for paper because they provide cellulose fibers in a much more usable condition, and therefore require less chemical treatment. "Rag" papers are made from these fiber sources, and cost more than purified wood-pulp papers. Suitable papers for storage can be made from either wood or rag pulps. Neither one has a guarantee of inertness toward photographs, but the rag sources generally yield a stronger, more satisfactory paper or board. Where possible, paper made

entirely from cotton or linen should be used for storage enclosures.

When paper products from wood-fiber sources are used for the storage of photographs, it is important to choose products which have a high content of alpha-cellulose, a non-degraded form of cellulose most desirable for paper intended to be permanent. Special pulping techniques are needed to produce permanent, wood-fiber papers. All papers and boards used for enclosures should be free from lignin, a powerful cause of staining and fading during long-term storage. They should also be free from metal particles or reactive sulfur. Any dyes or colorants present should be tested for possible reactions with silver, gelatin, or albumen.

Although the image has faded overall due to various environmental causes, a lignin-containing over-mat has produced additional fading around the perimeter of this gelatin developing-out paper print. Parts of the image not covered by the over-mat show less fading.

James M. Reilly

Another property of papers and boards which may affect their suitability as storage materials is the presence or absence of alkaline buffering. Acidity has been shown to contribute to the discoloration and embrittlement of paper, so many papers and boards intended for archival use contain substances to neutralize acidity. Calcium carbonate is the standard buffering agent, and buffered papers and boards may contain up to 3% calcium carbonate by weight.

Although alkaline buffering is stipulated in the requirements for paper enclosures for black-and-white photographs in ANSI Standard PH 1.53-1984, it may not be suitable for all types of 19th-century photographic prints. Cyanotypes should probably not be stored in direct contact with alkaline-buffered enclosures because their blue image can be bleached by alkaline conditions. Non-buffered enclosures have been recommended for albumen prints because one of the albumen yellowing reactions may be affected by alkaline conditions.[31] More recent research indicates that calcium carbonate buffering by itself does not significantly affect albumen prints.[56] A prudent course while awaiting the outcome of further research is to choose non-buffered enclosures for albumen prints, bearing in mind that the buffering question is minor when compared to the damage that could result from the presence of peroxides, lignin, or sulfur. Some platinotypes may actually benefit from buffered enclosures because their paper supports are often acidic and embrittled.

Under most environmental circumstances, buffering agents will not interact with prints (very high RH and direct contact are required). Moreover, the issue of buffering, in and of itself, is not significant enough to warrant replacing existing enclosures. A cautious general recommendation for 19th-century photographic prints (with exceptions as noted) is to use high quality non-buffered papers until the influence of alkaline-buffered enclosures on each print type is more fully explored. Non-buffered paper and boards made expressly for photographic storage are available from suppliers of archival materials.

Its designation as acid-free does not necessarily mean that a paper or board product contains alkaline buffering; it merely indicates that at the time of its manufacture the product contained no detectable acidity. (Most acid-free papers and boards do, however, contain some degree of alkaline buffering.) The term acid-free generally indicates that a paper product will be more permanent than ordinary grades of paper, but does not guarantee that it will be safe to use in photographic storage.

The same general guidelines apply in selecting mat boards or boards to produce additional support for prints inside sleeves, because boards are constructed by laminating layers of paper. The terminology used to describe the quality of board products, however, is somewhat different from that used for papers. Three types of mat board are sold: rag board, con-

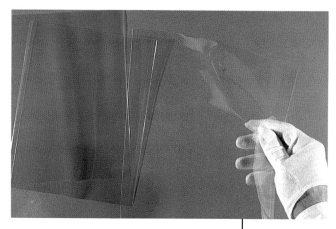

Transparent plastic sleeves of cellulose triacetate (or other suitable plastics) provide surface protection for prints, yet allow them to be viewed without removal from their enclosure.

James M. Reilly

servation board, and standard board. Rag boards are made from cotton and linen fiber sources, while conservation boards are made from high quality purified wood pulp. Standard boards are the lowest grade and usually contain significant amounts of lignin. They should *never* be used in the storage of 19th-century photographic prints.

Choosing Plastic Enclosure Materials

Three plastic enclosure materials are generally regarded as being safe for storing photographs: cellulose triacetate, polyester (polyethylene terephthalate), and polyethylene.[57] Cellulose triacetate and polyester have both been used extensively as support materials for photographic films, so their suitability for use in close contact with photographs has been well established. Any plastic material used in enclosure construction should be free from surface coatings and not contain an excessive amount of plasticizer. Polyvinyl chloride (PVC), "shrinkwrap," and highly chlorinated or nitrated plastic should be avoided. To be sure of quality, it is best to purchase plastics from photographic manufacturers or dealers in archival materials and to buy them in sheets or rolls, or prefabricated into sleeves, folders, or other formats.

DESIGN AND CONSTRUCTION OF ENCLOSURES

There are a number of enclosure styles for storing 19th-century photographic prints. Ideally there should be three levels of protection: the individual housing, a box, and a metal cabinet or shelf arrangement. For the sake of efficiency, each level should be designed to accommodate the others. One choice for an individual enclosure is to house prints in sleeves of cellulose triacetate or polyester, backing the print with a sheet of suitable board or heavy paper stock to lend support and provide additional physical protection. The print should be securely attached to the backing board[35] using one of the methods shown on page 100.

Plastic sleeves provide excellent protection, and their transparency allows the prints to be examined without being directly handled. They are available in a variety of sizes. It is best to choose a size slightly larger than the dimensions of the print or mount to be enclosed.

The additional supporting sheet of board or heavy paper stock should completely fill the sleeve, leaving a margin where cataloging information or any information from the back of the photograph can be copied. A danger associated with plastic sleeves is the possibility that at very high RH conditions they may adhere to or modify the surface of prints with gelatin binders. This is of less concern with albumen binders, which do not become as soft as gelatin in high moisture conditions. Polyester has a tendency to build up a slight electrostatic charge which is not normally a problem. When the enclosure directly covers a photograph which has charcoal or pastel applied to its surface, however, a polyester enclosure should not be used.

Another desirable approach to housing individual prints is to place them in a window mat of rag or other high quality board. (The construction of mats is described in Chapter VII.) This approach is more costly than plastic sleeves but offers advantages for some types of collections. Mats serve two purposes: they are a protective housing during storage and they allow a print to be displayed in a frame. When used as a storage enclosure, a thin sheet of uncoated polyester should be placed inside the mat to cover and protect the print surface.

Matting is an efficient style of enclosure for prints with a high artifact value or those likely to be exhibited several times. Mat sizes can be standardized to simplify boxing and shelving arrangements and to allow frames to be reused more efficiently. The physical support and protection offered by mats is excellent. Coupled with sturdy, inert boxes and suitable cabinets, matting is very satisfactory for storing prints. Its disadvantages are the high cost of materials, the labor required to construct mats, and the bulkiness of a matted collection.

There are many other possible styles of individual enclosures, including simple folders, envelopes, and encapsulation, in which a photograph is placed on a board of suitable quality and covered with a polyester sheet. (Some prints with very strong and secure original mounts may be totally encased in polyester.) Originally developed for paper documents, the encapsulation technique has several variants, but all seal the top and bottom pieces of encapsulating material with archival-quality, double-sided tape or by welding them with microwave radiation or ultrasound. The sealed perimeter extends nearly all the way around the print, quite close to its edge, and ensures that the print will not shift inside its protective housing. Encapsulation is best suited to prints which will be frequently handled, or which need extra protection during shipment. Whatever style or construction of enclosure is used to store a collection, all of the construction materials, including any adhesive used, should be of known quality and previously tested for their effects on photographs.

Much of the deterioration that is now evident in collections of 19th-century prints stems from their original mounting and enclosure materials. Because much of the original housing (mounts, adhesives, and album pages) must often remain with prints, part of the function of enclosures is to protect prints from each other. Even if no other type of enclosure is provided, interleaving prints with a suitable plastic or paper material is highly desirable. Interleaving book or album pages to protect photographs from migrating contaminants may be desirable, but is not always possible. Very thin polyester seems best for this purpose, but interleaving always adds bulk and may strain bindings. The decision to interleave pages in albums or books should be made for each individual case, based on a comparison of the need—the urgency of avoiding possible contamination or physical problems such as abrasion—and the effect of interleaving on the binding and aesthetics of the object. Interleaving requires that users be careful and conscientious during handling because folded interleaving can be destructive. All of these factors should be weighed before deciding to interleave book or album pages.

Albums and books should be provided with a sturdy and close-fitting protective housing.[58] Custom-made boxes of good quality, heavy paper stock are usually satisfactory for storing small albums, and can be constructed from two pieces of paper stock held together with cotton twill tape. Greater protection for objects of high artifact value can be provided by other two-piece box styles or by custom-made clamshell boxes.

STORAGE BOXES

Storage boxes constitute the second level of protective packaging. Just as each photograph should have its own individual enclosure, each photograph should be stored in a box to be shielded from dust, light, and physical damage. The materials used to make boxes should all be inert toward photographs.

Three types of boxes are in common use. The least costly are "document boxes" made from heavy paper stock held together at the corners with enameled steel fasteners. Several designs are available, including a flat-lidded, two-piece, drop-front style, and an upright, one-piece, "flip-top style." Care must be taken in selecting document boxes because the quality of their paper stock can vary from acceptable to quite unacceptable. It is important that the box material be free from lignin.

"Portfolio boxes" cost more than document boxes but provide more attractive and secure storage. Usually of one-piece clamshell construction, portfolio boxes are made from binder's board with a cloth covering. Their lining may be of either paper or spun-bonded polyethylene.

The third and most costly style of box is the "museum case" made with cloth-covered wooden sides for maximum strength and rigidity. Several variants of this general design are available, and this type of box has been used by museums for many years to house prints. Although the use of wood is questionable, under favorable environmental circumstances, the boxes appear to be safe.

A general principle in boxing prints is to match the sizes of prints and their enclosures as closely as possible to the dimensions of the box so as to minimize damage from the shifting of the prints. When prints are stored in a much larger box, groups of prints can be placed in a folder of suitable heavy paper stock or separated by dividers of thick board. Boxes should never be over-packed because of the resultant physical stresses on the prints and the need to handle many more prints than necessary. Clamshell-type boxes, in which the top and one side open out to form a flat surface, also eliminate the need to pry prints up by the edges during removal from the box.

VERTICAL STORAGE

Although horizontal storage in boxes is generally the most desirable and secure form of storage (especially for prints of high value or which are larger than 8 x 10 in.), vertical storage can be satisfactory in a properly designed filing system.[55] Each print should be individually housed and given a rigid backing. Folders are generally necessary, and the number of prints in each folder should be kept small. The most important aspect of vertical storage is to provide rigid dividers in the file drawer to prevent damage from sagging or flexing; they should be no more than six to eight inches apart. All materials used for enclosures and dividers should be suitable for use with photographs, and the filing cabinets should be metal with a baked-enamel finish.

SHELVING AND CABINETS

The ideal arrangement for storing boxed prints consists of closed metal cabinets with deep shelving to accommodate one layer (or, at most, two layers) of boxes on each shelf. Metal with a baked-enamel finish is the preferred construction material for shelving. Unfinished wood or plywood is the least desirable[59] because wood releases harmful peroxides and other organic vapors. Some types of wood finishes release oxidant gases as they cure, and the effectiveness of a finish as a seal against contamination from wood itself is very difficult to evaluate. It is prudent to avoid wooden cabinets and shelving altogether, despite the appeal of fine wooden cabinetry.

The design of cabinets and shelving should make it easy to insert and remove boxes of prints. Heavy boxes on high shelves can be difficult to handle and can endanger the prints and the collection staff. A step stool should be provided where shelves are slightly too high for convenient access while standing. The shelving arrangements for large boxes, particularly those housing heavy albums or books, should allow for two people to work together when inserting or removing a box. Aisles in storage areas should be wide enough to allow plenty of room for print removal and easy access by transportation carts.

STORAGE SITES

Choosing where to store 19th-century prints is easiest when a new or extensively renovated facility is being planned because the layout of storage and work areas can then be integrated with an efficient environmental control system. In a new facility, the fewest compromises of convenience, security, and expansion room need be made.

Some compromises are inevitable when a storage site must be selected within an existing structure, but areas with difficult environmental problems should be avoided regardless of their other attractive features. Attics or any area directly under a roof are subject to extremes of temperature and quite rapid temperature changes. Such a site is unsuitable without insulation and controls for temperature and humidity. Attic-stored material is also vulnerable to water damage from leaking roofs.

Photographs should not be stored in basements. The coolness found in basements tends to make them damp, and articles stored there are prone to water damage from several other sources, including burst pipes, sewer back-ups, and the seepage of groundwater through walls during heavy rains. During a general flood, the basement is the most vulnerable location within a structure.

Localized environmental problems are not confined to attics and basements. Exterior walls are sometimes cool enough to create a damp zone near the wall. In general, locations along exterior walls, especially near radiators or windows, should not be used as storage sites. There can be temperature and humidity gradients within rooms: boxes on high shelves close to ceilings can experience hotter and drier conditions than boxes closer to the floor. Avoid locations traversed by water, drain, or steam pipes, or those underneath sinks or toilet facilities on floors above.[60]

Chapter VII:

HANDLING, DISPLAY, AND CARE

The condition of most 19th-century photographs now found in collections clearly shows that the kind of care prints need is not what they typically get. Signs of improper handling, prolonged or ill-prepared display, and unwise "care" are plainly evident in all but a few collections.

This chapter describes the correct handling and display practices for 19th-century photographic prints and discusses principles of proper care and conservation. These are all part of the normal life of a photograph in a collection, but can also imperil a print if not done cautiously, conscientiously, and knowledgeably.

HANDLING

DANGERS OF IMPROPER HANDLING

Because handling is such a frequent cause of print deterioration, it is important to understand how to minimize its dangers. Few people fully realize how much the prints in collections are actually handled. Many hands touch a print as it is registered, cataloged, copied, matted, framed, or replaced in storage, as well as during its use for research. A print can also be handled often during searches for other images.

A print is at risk each time it is handled. Finger oils are acidic, attract dirt, and can deteriorate silver images and binder layers. Although clean hands are obviously required, prints themselves are often dirty and can soil hands, which then spread dirt to other prints. But the chief dangers of handling are physical; prints have almost no ability to withstand blows, flexing, or abrasion. Without extra protection from enclosures and deliberate, careful handling, prints have little chance of surviving intact.

The physical dangers of handling arise from the nature of prints as paper objects and from their character as laminates of dissimilar materials.[35] The paper supports of nearly all types of 19th-century photographic prints are thinner than those of modern photographic prints, and their binders are usually either inherently brittle or have become brittle with age. Unmounted prints, especially those on thin paper, are unable to support their own weight and are difficult to handle safely. Albumen prints, with their flexible supports and rather brittle albumen layers, are a particular problem in this regard. They should be grasped with both hands and supported properly to avoid creasing. The common one-handed grasp, with thumb above and fingers below, has caused semicircular creases in innumerable prints. Unmounted prints are also especially vulnerable to tears (usually along the lines of earlier creases), crumpling, and folding. They are often tightly curled; in this condition, they should only be dealt with by a conservator.

Mounted prints are often brittle and inflexible. Mounting provides support but also bonds the print to its mount. The quality of mounting boards varies, but a significant number have become extremely brittle with age. If not grasped with both hands and supported properly, there is a danger that the mount will fracture and tear the print. Attention to the signs of brittle supports and mounts is an important part of safe handling.

Large prints, being unwieldy and difficult to grasp properly, present another set of handling problems. Their weight makes it especially important that they be supported at all times. The danger of creasing and tearing increases with the size of a print. Very large prints should be supported and guided by two people working together. Large albums or books can be quite heavy, and unless their weight is carefully managed, it is all too easy to break their spines. Oversize albums and books can be more safely handled in custom-made boxes.

SAFE HANDLING

It is essential to make all those who handle collection materials aware of the need for care at all times. Safe handling involves skills acquired through experience, through knowledge of the potential dangers, and—perhaps most importantly—through developing an attitude of caution and deliberation. Experienced handlers proceed slowly; no matter what their immediate purpose in handling an object, they never lose sight of the delicate physical nature of prints or albums.

Basic safe handling practices include having clean hands together with a clean and adequately large workspace. Print surfaces should never be touched, and prints should be handled firmly but gently with both hands. White cotton gloves are often recommended to reduce the finger marking of mats and other types of enclosures. Gloves reduce manual dexterity and can become soiled, but are beneficial when prints are well-housed and full dexterity is not required for safe handling.

Protective packaging is obviously an important factor in minimizing handling damage. The types of storage enclosures and housing recommended in Chapter VI also provide a rigid support and protection for the print surface during handling. Prints should never be integrated into storage or handled for any purpose without a protective enclosure, and care should always be taken when placing prints in enclosures, particularly plastic sleeves. Access to damaged or especially fragile items should be restricted until their condition is stabilized by a conservator.

Beyond educating handlers (including staff) and providing protective enclosures, handling damage can be minimized by avoiding all but essential handling of valuable original prints. Thoughtful organization of collection procedures will ensure that prints are not handled unnecessarily during registration, cataloging, and reproduction. Copy negatives and prints should be substituted for originals whenever possible. For complete information on this subject, refer to KODAK Publication M-1, *Copying and Duplicating*. When original prints are required, adequate time should be given to locate and prepare them for examination.[43]

DISPLAY

The safe display of 19th-century photographic prints requires adequate preparation, an understanding of how light and the environment affect prints, and a sense of caution. Each of the various print materials has individual characteristics which affect its ability to withstand the rigors of display. Before exhibiting any print, read in Chapters II and III about the specific components and characteristic forms of deterioration which occur in that type of print.

The decision to display a 19th-century photographic print should not be made lightly or routinely. Display involves considerable handling and introduces a new and harsher set of environmental conditions. Consider each print not only as a representative of a print "type," but as a unique artifact. For one reason or another, many prints should not be displayed. A deteriorated print may be unable to withstand handling or exposure to light during exhibition. Some rare and unusual types of paper prints, especially very early or experimental ones, may still be light-sensitive. If there is any uncertainty about a print's ability to bear up to display, do not exhibit it. It is better to err on the side of caution than to risk damaging a valuable original.

Examine each object considered for display for any component that may be light-sensitive. Applied color or albumen tinting dyes are obvious examples, but some assemblages have unusual components which are photosensitive, such as dyed fabrics. The decision whether or not to exhibit a given print should also be influenced by the nature of the exhibition arrangements. It is not always possible to display prints under optimal environmental and lighting conditions (see pages 102–106). If light levels, RH, or temperature conditions are not optimal, the selection of images for display should be made more conservatively and display times should be strictly limited.

MATTING AND FRAMING PRACTICES

The first step in preparing a print for exhibition is to secure it inside a window mat.[61] A mat is a protective folder made by binding together two pieces of high quality board. The print is securely attached to the bottom board and is visible through an opening in the upper board. The mat provides an attractive, inert, and secure housing for the print inside a frame, and keeps it from touching the glass. A mat can also serve as a useful storage enclosure if a sheet of thin polyester (or other suitable material) is placed inside to cover and protect the print surface.

There are many mat styles and many methods for securing prints inside mats. A complete discussion of matting and framing practices is beyond the scope of this book. Consult the references in the bibliography for greater detail. Only the rudiments of matting and framing will be presented here, and emphasis will be placed on the quality of the materials used and on the elements of design and construction which most influence the safety of prints.

Matting

All of the materials and adhesives used in the construction of mats should be of the highest quality and meet the same standards of inertness toward photographs required for storage materials (see Chapter VI). Variations in matting materials and matting designs may be aesthetically appealing, but may also involve the use of materials unsuited for contact with photographs. Fabrics, pressure-sensitive tapes, adhesives of unknown quality, and highly colored boards[56] should all be avoided in mat-

ting 19th-century photographic prints. For a complete discussion of these materials, see KODAK Publication F-40, *Conservation of Photographs*.

Mats should be constructed with standard outer dimensions that complement the sizes of storage boxes and shelving. Two-ply boards are safe for small mats, but are not rigid enough to safely support large prints; four-ply board should be used for mats 11 x 14 in. (28.6 x 36.2 cm) or larger. Any marks made on the upper board as guides for cutting the window opening should be drawn with a pencil and erased before assembling the mat to keep them from being transferred to the print or its mount. The cutting of the window opening creates a sharp edge on the mat board which can damage the print. Burnishing the edge of the bevel with a bone folder (a special-purpose tool used in book binding), so that the cut edge does not contact the print, will eliminate this danger. Before assembling the mat, all eraser crumbs and dust should be removed. The top and bottom pieces of the mat should be bound together with a non-acid linen tape. The tape should never be in contact with the print, and should run nearly the entire length of the mat's longest dimension.

There are several ways to secure a print to a mat; three are shown in the figure below. Whichever method is used, it is essential that the attachment be fully able to support the weight of both the print and its mount.

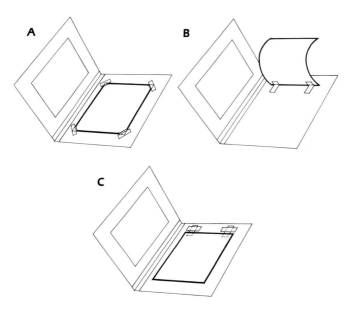

A   B

C

Attachment Styles

Three possible approaches to adhering prints to window mats are shown in this sketch.

Constance McCabe

When a print has a mount with a generous border area, or when an unmounted print has a wide border, the best way to attach the print to the backing board is with folded corners of high quality paper or polyester, as shown in Attachment Style A. This has the advantage of not requiring any adhesives in contact with the print or its mount. The corners are secured to the backing board with a strip of linen tape running across them and onto the board.

The corners should fit loosely and be as large as possible without touching the image area of the print. Corners which are too small are a hazard, and another attachment method is needed when it is not possible to create corners large enough to fully support the print. The weight of a very large, unmounted, and flexible print will cause buckling, regardless of the corner size. Such prints should be attached with hinges (see below) or a combination of hinges and corners. When removing prints from folded corners, the tape holding the corners should be carefully cut with a scalpel to avoid the risk of damaging the print by bending it during removal.

Another method of attachment is with hinges of long-fibered Japanese tissue, as shown in the second and third sketches. Thin strips of the tissue are adhered with wheat starch paste to the back of the print or its mount and to the backing board of the mat. Two hinge styles are commonly used: a folded hinge (Style B) and a reinforced "T" style (Style C). Which is chosen will depend on the weight of the print and on whether or not the entire print is to be visible through the window opening. Hinging with Japanese tissue is a very satisfactory method of attachment, but it puts adhesives in contact with prints or their mounts. The moisture of the adhesive can cockle prints with thin supports, such as unmounted albumen prints.[55] Although seemingly simple, hinging with Japanese tissue requires skill and practice.

No matter which attachment method is used, a sheet of thin polyester slightly smaller than the mat itself should be placed inside it to protect the print surface during handling and storage. The corners of the polyester sheet should be rounded to prevent snagging. It is also good practice to copy in pencil inside the mat (or on its reverse) any inscription or written information which is on the mount or reverse of the print, so that subsequent removal or lifting of the print is not necessary.[43] If no inscription exists, that, too, should be noted.

Framing

The framing materials used to display 19th-century photographic prints can significantly protect or harm the prints. Frames are essential to protect prints on exhibition from dust, atmospheric contamination, and theft; they can also substantially reduce photochemical damage. In general, the safest frames are the metal-section type because, unlike wood frames, they do not have the potential for releasing peroxides and organic vapors. When wooden frames are used, raw wood or freshly-finished frames should be avoided. It is prudent to seal the "rabbet" (the groove or channel behind the face of the frame molding) of wooden frames with a polyester-film tape to keep harmful vapors from entering into the mat package.

Picture glass or acrylic plastic sheeting are both acceptable glazing materials. Glass filters out some of the most harmful wavelengths of ultraviolet radiation (UV), but greater protection is desirable. Some acrylic glazing materials filter out all but a very small portion of UV, making them the preferred material for use in displaying 19th-century prints. Acrylics, being shatterproof, are very useful in traveling exhibitions but are easily scratched and more costly than glass. Their higher cost, however, is justified by the protection they offer against UV.

It is a good practice before framing a print to create a sealed package consisting of the glazing material, the matted sheet, and a backing sheet of polyester so that the mat is sandwiched between two vapor-impermeable materials.[55] To avoid trapping moisture inside, the package should be assembled under recommended conditions of relative humidity. Be sure that all components have had sufficient time to equilibrate to those conditions. The edges of the package should be sealed with a polyester film or other suitable archival-quality tape. The tape should only slightly overlap the glazing material in order to be concealed under the lip of the frame molding. When prints are framed for a traveling exhibition or when environmental conditions in an exhibition area are not optimal, a sealed package can shield prints from fluctuating or harmful environmental conditions.

DISPLAY OF ALBUMS AND BOOKS

Many 19th-century photographic prints are found in albums or books and therefore cannot be matted and framed for display. In the past, the practice of dismantling books and albums to conveniently exhibit the photographs they contained was unfortunately widespread. More recently, the importance of keeping albums and books as integral entities has been recognized, and efforts have been made to display prints in their original context.

Showcases are required to display albums and books. Each showcase contains a micro-climate which only slowly interchanges with the room environment. The pollutant levels and conditions of temperature and RH in a display case may differ significantly from general room conditions.[59] Radiant heating or lights inside showcases can raise temperatures and lower humidities. The choice of materials for showcase construction is especially important because the harmful vapors some materials release can reach dangerous concentrations inside a closed case. The safe materials for showcase construction are those recommended for storage enclosures and framing materials: metal, glass, acrylic sheeting, cotton, and linen. Avoid using wool, polyurethane foams, unknown adhesives, and oil-base paints. Woods and some types of wood finishes can release harmful vapors, so their use in showcase construction should be avoided. Exposed wood inside showcases should be sealed with polyester film and a conservation quality polyvinylacetate adhesive.

Damage to the spine of an open album or book may result if it is rested flat inside a showcase. A custom-made cradle for support in the appropriate position should be provided. When cradling open books or albums at an incline, avoid damage from sagging pages by using a loop of polyester film to hold the pages in place.

THE DISPLAY ENVIRONMENT

The display environment is more rigorous than the storage environment because it adds the potential for light-induced damage to all of the other environmental circumstances. The following discussion emphasizes the effects of light on prints, but it should not be forgotten that prints on exhibition are still subject to the environmentally-induced forms of deterioration that affect them in dark storage. Indeed, the harmful effects of light are made much worse under conditions of high temperature and humidity, and lead to greater deterioration than either the environmental conditions or light would produce on their own.

The recommended environmental conditions for display are the same as those for storage: 30-40% RH, and temperatures under 18°C (65°F). Avoid displaying prints on cool outside walls or directly over radiators or hot air registers. Use latex paints to prepare walls and display areas because peroxides are emitted during the curing of oil-base paints.[21]

Appropriate display of 19th-century photographic prints includes environmental controls, proper lighting, and the use of safe framing materials. All these elements are combined in the photographic galleries of the Art Institute of Chicago.

Art Institute of Chicago

102

LIGHT

Light is quite obviously indispensable for displaying photographic prints; thus it is essential to understand the nature of light and how it can influence the deterioration of photographs.[62] Light is a form of radiant energy. It contributes the energy needed to set in motion the chemical reactions that cause decay and discoloration. Light is only a small part of the continuous spectrum of radiant energy which includes x-rays, ultraviolet radiation, visible light, and infrared radiation. Visible light is the kind of radiation to which human vision is sensitive.

All forms of radiation have wavelike properties, so it is convenient to classify them on the basis of wavelength. The dispersion of sunlight with a prism separates visible light into a spectrum which ranges from the shortest wavelengths (violet) to the longest (red). At wavelengths shorter than visible light lies *ultraviolet radiation*, while at wavelengths longer than visible light is *infrared radiation*. There is a relationship between the wavelength of radiation and the energy that it possesses: the shorter the wavelength the more energetic it is, and the more likely to cause chemical reactions. Ultraviolet light therefore causes far greater deterioration than visible light. Within the visible spectrum, blue light has more energy than green, and green more than red. Infrared radiation is weaker still, and does not directly cause photochemical change; its main effect is to raise the temperature of materials which absorb it. But it is important to emphasize that visible light as well as UV can cause photochemical damage and that *protection from UV does not eliminate the danger of light damage.*

PHOTOCHEMICAL DAMAGE TO PRINTS

The substances most affected by light damage tend to be organic materials, both natural and synthetic—the very components of photographic prints. Cellulose is embrittled (and discolored if lignin is present) by exposure to light. Proteins are also affected, though albumen is much more sensitive to photochemical deterioration than gelatin. Light causes albumen to yellow. Perhaps the most photosensitive of all components of 19th-century

The organic dyes used in the manufacture of albumen paper gave this print an overall pink coloration in the highlights. The extreme sensitivity of these dyes to photochemical damage can be seen from this example which was displayed for only a few weeks under tungsten illumination. The pink dye has been bleached by light everywhere except where it was protected by an overmat.

Sergio Burgi, IMP/GEH

prints are organic dyes, particularly those used to give an overall pink or purple cast to albumen prints.[30] Even inorganic watercolor pigments are photosensitive when present as thin surface washes, and extra caution should be observed in setting light levels and display times for any print with applied color.

When poor quality papers and boards that contain lignin are irradiated, the lignin undergoes photochemical reactions and produces substances that stain prints and attack silver images. The damage produced by all forms of photochemical deterioration is cumulative and generally irreversible. The best way to minimize such damage is to use light sources that contain a low proportion of the shorter, more energetic wavelengths, and to limit the duration of exposure to light.

Prints can also be damaged by light during photocopying. The duration and intensity of illumination used in making photographic copies is normally not harmful, but prints can be damaged if copied on electrostatic copying machines. Such copiers expose prints to considerable heat and UV radiation and should not be used to copy original 19th-century prints.

LIGHT SOURCES FOR DISPLAY

Tungsten Incandescent Lamps

An ideal light source for illuminating prints would produce only visible radiation, with no ultraviolet or infrared output. It would have a smaller proportion of shorter-wavelength blue light than the less harmful green and red wavelengths. Regrettably, such an ideal light source does not exist. The best choice among the commonly available light sources is the tungsten incandescent lamp, which produces light by heating a tungsten filament to incandescence inside a glass envelope. Tungsten lamps are familiar to everyone as the ordinary incandescent light bulb and are sold in many forms for exhibition lighting.

Tungsten lamps produce little ultraviolet radiation, and their blue light output is smaller than their green and red output. While tungsten light seems yellow in comparison with daylight or fluorescent light, its "warmth" does not seriously affect the appreciation of color. In fact, at the low light levels recommended for the display of prints, "warm" illumination has the psychological effect of seeming cheerful and welcoming. Diffuse daylight at the same levels is often perceived as being gloomy and vaguely unsettling.[63]

Most of the electrical energy consumed by tungsten lamps is converted to heat which warms the lamp and reflector. In addition, tungsten lamps produce a high level of infrared radiation. At recommended RH levels, the main danger from radiant heating is the drying of objects rather than the influence of temperature on chemical reactions. At the recommended levels of illumination for prints, there is little to fear from the infrared output of tungsten lamps.

Sunlight and Daylight

Direct sunlight and daylight contain a much higher proportion of UV radiation than tungsten light does; they cannot be used to illuminate prints without being filtered to remove their UV component. For several reasons, it is extremely difficult to use safely natural light as the main source of display illumination. The levels of light entering a room through a window or skylight vary tremendously and continually. As the position of the sun changes, the illumination changes in direction as well as in intensity. In order to achieve recommended levels, natural light must normally be highly attenuated and diffused, which affects the perception of surface texture.

In addition to being impractical as the primary source of display illumination, natural light from windows and skylights in the display area requires special attention. A first step in dealing with light from windows and skylights is to cover them with UV filters which are sold in the form of self-adhesive plastic films. The overall light levels inside the room should also be controlled with venetian blinds or shades on the upper halves of windows, and with net curtains and other barriers. Direct sunlight should not be allowed to fall on prints, and the positioning of prints on the walls should be carefully chosen to minimize the amount of illumination received from windows or skylights. The most fully satisfactory solution in dealing with natural light is usually to eliminate it from the display area altogether. When that is not possible, it is important to take all possible measures to ameliorate the dangers it poses to photographic prints.

Fluorescent Lamps

There are many different types of fluorescent lamps, but most have a significant output of UV radiation and must therefore be filtered when used to illuminate prints. Plastic shields which remove UV and fit over fluorescent tubes are sold for this purpose, and filtration may also be incorporated into diffusing panels in lamp fixtures. Different types of fluorescent lamps vary in their effect on the appreciation of color, and they are more inconvenient than tungsten lamps for lighting or displaying prints because their output is not easily focused and directed.

MEASURING LIGHT LEVELS

Although the human visual system can adapt to a wide range of light levels, it is not very good at objectively measuring them. Consequently, we must rely on instruments to ascertain whether illumination is at safe levels. The light-measuring devices normally used in museums and galleries are balanced to measure light as the human eye perceives it: they are most sensitive to green light and do not "see" UV or infrared at all. Portable, battery-operated devices are available that simply and reliably measure *illuminance*, the amount of light falling on the photosensitive probe of the instrument.

The unit of illuminance is the *lux* (*lx*). Sometimes light levels are measured or expressed in *foot-candles* (*fc*), an older English unit which has been replaced by the lux. There are approximately 10 lux to each foot-candle. In measuring the light levels for a display of photographic prints, a light meter graduated in lux should be used. The sensor of the measuring instrument should be held parallel to and quite near the surface of the print. Care must be taken to ensure that no light is blocked by the person doing the measurement. Several readings should be made, especially on large prints.

In some circumstances, it may be desirable to measure the ultraviolet radiation reaching prints on display or in work areas. This is not necessary when an exhibition is lighted entirely with tungsten illumination at recommended levels because the proportion of UV radiation in the output of tungsten lamps is low. When it is necessary to measure the proportion of UV radiation in incident light, it can be done with relatively inexpen-

sive portable equipment, much as visible light is measured. The units for expressing the proportion of UV radiation are microwatts per lumen (μW/lm). A value of about 75 μW/lm (roughly the same proportion as produced by conventional tungsten lamps) should not be exceeded.

RECOMMENDED LIGHT LEVELS FOR DISPLAY

For visible light, the recommended maximum level of illumination for displaying most types of 19th-century prints is 50 lux (5 foot-candles). This is the internationally accepted standard for the illumination of vulnerable materials, including prints and drawings, textiles, and natural-history specimens.[64] The 50-lux standard applies to all photographic print materials that have exposed paper fibers (salted paper prints, platinotypes, cyanotypes, gum bichromate prints, and carbon prints), to all photomechanical print materials, and to albumen prints. It also applies to all prints that have applied color in any form. Prints with baryta coatings (most gelatin developing-out papers, gelatin printing-out papers, and collodion printing-out papers) may tolerate up to 100 lux (10 foot-candles).

It should be noted that these illumination levels have not been experimentally established for each print process, but are extrapolated from the recommendations for works of art on paper and from experience with the individual components of prints rather than the photographic materials themselves. However, the effects of photochemical damage on the component materials of prints are quite well established.

Photographic prints can be adequately seen and appreciated when illuminated at the 50-lux level, but a problem can arise if visitors encounter an exhibit without having had a chance to adapt their vision to the low light level. People coming from outdoors or from a brightly-lighted part of a building need up to several minutes to fully adapt to low levels of illumination. Adaptation may be encouraged in a number of ways, notably by routing visitors who are approaching the exhibition area through rooms and corridors with successively lower light levels. It is also helpful to illuminate evenly the exhibition area at 50 lux and to avoid stark white or

---

LIGHTING CONDITIONS
FOR DISPLAY
OF 19TH-CENTURY
PHOTOGRAPHIC PRINTS

Use Tungsten Incandescent Lights

Light Levels For:

—Salted Paper Prints
—Albumen Prints
—Platinotypes
—Gum Bichromate Prints
—Carbon Prints
—Photomechanical Prints
—All Prints With Applied Color

50 Lux (5 Foot-Candles)

Light Levels For:

—Gelatin Printing-Out Papers
—Collodion Printing-Out Papers
—Gelatin Developing-Out
  Papers (B & W Prints)

100 Lux (10 Foot-Candles)

---

very dark walls. Tungsten incandescent lamps are the most practical and successful light source for 50-lux illumination.

DISPLAY TIME

The relative energy of light sources and intensity of illumination have been shown to be important considerations in protecting prints from photochemical damage while on display. There is a third significant factor: display time, or, more properly, illumination time. The best defense against photochemical damage to prints is to limit both display time and the intensity of illumination. This can be done in a number of ways. An obvious but important measure is to make sure that exhibitions are illuminated only when open to the public. For extra protection of sensitive objects, a simple expedient which has been successfully used is to place a cloth over a frame. A more refined but essentially similar approach is visitor-activated lighting turned on with a foot switch or photoelectric cell.

It is not possible to give specific, long-term maximum display times at recommended light levels for the various 19th-century photographic print processes. The most photosensitive type of print is a tinted albumen print with its tinting dye intact. Once the dye has faded, the print is no longer as sensitive to light, but, of course, is still subject to photochemical damage. Even at recommended levels of illumination, damage to tinted albumen prints may occur within a few weeks. Fortunately, not all prints are this sensitive to light damage; but in general, the display of prints should be kept to the minimum required for the educational or artistic purposes the photographs serve.

Prints should never be displayed on an indefinite basis, and it is a good practice to monitor the condition of prints at frequent intervals while they are on display. Gradual but dramatic changes can go unnoticed, so periodic visual inspection of the entire print is helpful. Photochemical damage is usually most apparent as a difference in appearance between exposed print areas and those protected by the overmat. More precise monitoring of changes during display can be done with a reflection densitometer, an instrument which measures the density (lightness or darkness) of the image of a photographic print.[65]

CARE

THE IMPORTANCE OF BASIC CARE AND STORAGE

The care of 19th-century photographic prints includes all measures taken to prevent further deterioration and to correct and repair damage that has already occurred. Such care is provided on two levels: by the owners and custodians of prints, and by conservation professionals. Curatorial care (that which is provided by the owners) is directed at the preservation of entire collections. It is concerned with environmental controls, protective packaging, and the safety of prints during handling and use. The level of care provided by conservation professionals can encompass curatorial care, but typically is directed much more toward prints as individual objects and includes conservation treatments to repair the effects of deterioration.

Although both levels of care are important, the survival of the cultural legacy of 19th-century photography depends mainly on the quality of *curatorial care* rather than on conservation treatment. All prints are greatly affected by their storage environment and are vulnerable to handling damage, but only a small minority will ever receive attention from a professional conservator. For most of the significant forms of deterioration in prints—image oxidation, sulfiding, and binder damage—no safe and effective restoration treatment now exists. The greatest preservation challenge for the foreseeable future will be to identify those prints that are culturally significant and provide them with the basic care and storage conditions they need to survive.

CURATORIAL CARE

The essence of care, whether provided by the curator or the professional conservator, is knowledge. Much harm has been done to prints in the name of preservation by those who, with the best of intentions, had too little knowledge of the nature of prints and the consequences of the "treatments" they were attempting. In most collections, one does not have to look very hard to find evidence of damage from improper mounting, rubber cement, cellophane tapes, and from many other causes related to care and conservation.

The information and procedures that constitute sound curatorial care for 19th-century photographic prints are presented throughout this book. However, an important part of taking proper care of prints is understanding what not to do and appreciating the limits of responsible intervention for curatorial care. Many prints need restraint or additional physical support to prevent curling and flexing, but the overall adhering of prints to a secondary support by any method is the province of a professional photographic conservator. "Dry mounting" with heat-set tissue is generally to be avoided with 19th-century prints because of the ill effects of heat and pressure and the difficulty of disassembling dry-mounted prints.

All restoration treatments should be done by trained conservation professionals. The effects of simple immersion in water can be serious and unpredictable.[35] Water immersion can cause binder damage, irreversible dimensional change, damage to applied color and retouching, migration of contaminants, and heightened chemical reactivity in all print components. Under no circumstances should attempts be made to intensify or chemically restore silver images, de-acidify supports, or bleach stains unless done by a trained photographic conservator. Likewise, the relaxation of tightly curled prints, mending of tears and missing areas, cleaning of print surfaces, and restoration of the image by retouching cannot be done safely without specialized knowledge and extensive experience.

Such intervention is obviously risky and well beyond the limits of sound curatorial care. It is less easy to define the limits of curatorial care for minor remedial treatments: dusting, cleaning mount surfaces, dealing with folded or crumpled prints, and constructing special packaging for odd or problem objects.

Even such minor remedial treatments, which may appear simple and safe, can do more harm than good without a sound understanding of the principles behind them. Inexperienced people usually underestimate the difficulties of both major and minor remedial treatment and attempt procedures which are either inherently unsafe or beyond their ability. Minor remedial treatments can be done safely by owners or custodians of prints, but only with guidance from a conservation professional or with a working knowledge of the literature of photographic conservation. There is information available in the literature of paper and photographic conservation that can help a curator or archivist safely perform minor cleaning and housing procedures,[66] but sources should be carefully chosen. Perspectives on the care of photographs have changed in recent years, and much of the literature on photographs was not written from a conservation viewpoint. Perhaps the most satisfactory approach in mastering minor remedial treatments is to combine a program of ongoing self-education with occasional consultation from a conservation professional.

CARE BY A CONSERVATOR

A tradition of art restoration by skilled craftspeople has existed for centuries, but within the last few decades the conservation profession has changed dramatically. It has grown in size and become a community of professionals who combine scientific, art-historical, and restoration skills to preserve and restore cultural property. However, only very recently has there emerged a branch of the conservation profession devoted specifically to photographs.[67]

It is useful for the owners and custodians of 19th-century photographic prints to be aware of the nature of the conservation profession and the ways in which conservators work. When an object is referred to a conservator, nothing is done to it before it is carefully studied and analyzed. Treatment, if performed, will be based on this *technical examination*, which can include a wide variety of analytical techniques, such as microscopic examination, instrumental analysis, and visual inspection. Chemical testing with solvents and tests on tiny samples removed from the object may also be performed.

All of the information gained from the technical examination is written down and incorporated into a *condition report* (or *report of technical examination*), which records the size, physical attributes, forms and location of deterioration, and all of the other findings from the examination. This documentation both forms a record of the individual object and becomes a

The photographic conservation laboratory at the Art Institute of Chicago includes preparation and examination areas (top) and a deep sink and fumehood (bottom).

part of a collective data base from which much can subsequently be learned.

Technical photography is useful for recording the condition of objects before, during, and after treatment. It is always a good practice to make a photographic record of any object before performing conservation treatment. Photographs (sometimes utilizing the infrared and UV regions of the spectrum) can also be useful in analyzing an object and characterizing deterioration.

The next step is to formulate a *treatment proposal* based on the results of the technical examination and the conservator's understanding of the problem. A treatment proposal is also based on information provided by the curator or owner of an object: the value of the object, its historical or aesthetic significance, its practical use, and any previous conservation treatment. The detailed treatment proposal is written and submitted to the curator or owner, who then joins with the conservator to decide on a course of action for the object.

Two principles are generally followed in formulating a plan for conservation treatment. The first is reversibility, that is, the notion that everything done to the object may be undone without causing harm to it. Complete reversibility is desirable but not always possible. The second principle is to use only proven treatments, not experimental ones. This, too, is an ideal which is not always attainable in practice.

It is not at all uncommon for conservators and curators to decide not to proceed with treatment until an object can be studied further or until the particular problems involved are better understood. Few circumstances in any branch of conservation require "emergency" treatment, and photographic conservation is no exception. Like the owner or curator of a photograph, the conservator must assess his or her own ability and be cautious in deciding to intervene with photographs. In many cases, it is better to do what can be done to stabilize the object against further deterioration and not attempt restoration treatment at all.

After treatment is completed, a written statement of the work performed and the final condition of the

object is prepared. This document is known as a *treatment report*. In many instances, a treatment report also includes a brief statement on how to care for the object in the future, noting any special problems that still exist. Treatment reports are important because they form a permanent record which will later be consulted when information is needed about an object for either curatorial or conservation purposes. Records of conservation treatment are also significant for subsequent evaluation of the success or failure of procedures and materials used for restoration.

The Limits of the Conservation/ Restoration of Photographs

It is important for owners and custodians of 19th-century photographic prints to understand not only the approach of the conservation profession generally, but also something of the state of *photographic* conservation. In comparison to sculpture or oil painting, photography, in existence for only 150 years, is a relatively new medium. Only very recently has any serious attention been given to preserving photographic artifacts in their original form. For many years, copying was regarded as an acceptable way of preserving photographs; only when photographs began to command high prices in the art market did consideration begin to be given to their conservation. Our culture is now beginning to take photographs more seriously, both as information

sources and aesthetic objects. This has created a need for techniques useful in their conservation.

Because of its brief history, photographic conservation has not been able to develop effective treatment methods through trial and error. Instead, there exists for photographs a body of chemical treatments originally meant to correct for errors in processing. Largely unsuitable for use on valuable photographs, especially 19th-century photographic prints, these restoration treatments are unpredictable at best and ruinous at worst. Very few of them meet the standards of reversibility, reliability, and safety which are demanded of treatments in other conservation disciplines.

In fact, the repertoire of treatments available to the photographic conservator—much of it borrowed from paper conservation—is quite small and is applicable mainly to the binderless print materials like salted paper prints. Photographic prints are very complex in their structures and chemistry; among many other problems, the reactivity of silver images and the unpredictable behavior of binder materials like gelatin prevent the use of restoration techniques from other branches of conservation.

Owners and curators should realize some of the dangerous implications of the infant state of photographic conservation, and the enormous variety and complexity of restoration problems. First, given the present state of

While there is little that can be done to reverse severe yellowing and fading of albumen prints, treatment by a professional conservator can often do much to stabilize and improve the appearance of a damaged print. This example was treated at the Center for Conservation of Art and Historic Artifacts in Philadelphia, Pennsylvania. The print is shown before (left) and after treatment (right).

Courtesy of
Debbie Hess Norris and
Special Collections,
University of Maryland,
College Park Libraries

knowledge, radical treatments are likely to do much more harm than good. Secondly, as mentioned above, basic care and storage are ultimately more significant than conservation treatment in the survival of our photographic legacy. An awareness of the limitations of restoration only underscores the need to *prevent* further deterioration. Thirdly, curators and owners of prints should recognize that a photographic conservator's reluctance to treat chemically the basic forms of deterioration, such as image fading, yellowing, and binder damage, probably represents professionalism and experience rather than naive timidity. Although chemical restoration treatments are severely limited, the professional photographic conservator can do much mechanically to support and stabilize the condition of prints against further deterioration. This can save many prints and would be impossible without the professional conservator's high level of training and experience.

Finally, it should be realized that some of the problems of photographic conservation may never be satisfactorily solved. Whatever progress is made will come from a long period of applying scientific resources and human talent to the problem. Sustained, systematic research is the only hope for improving the present state of photographic conservation.

Collection Surveys

One of the most useful and important functions a conservation professional serves is that of advising those who provide curatorial care. This can be done through publications or meetings and seminars, but it is sometimes difficult to relate general advice to the individual circumstances of a given collection. If a conservator or photographic conservation specialist is not available on the staff of a collection, it is often advantageous to arrange for a visit and consultation by an outside professional.

In the course of a visit, a conservator can help with the identification of collection materials, assess the overall condition of the collection, make recommendations for storage and handling, and assist in establishing conservation priorities. Such a consultation is known as a *collection survey*, and usually includes a written report which is useful for future guidance and for obtaining administrative backing to implement the consultant's recommendations.

A collection survey can be a highly efficient way to improve rapidly the preservation policies of a collection. The consultant is not only armed with experience and knowledge, but brings a fresh perspective to a collection's problems. A consultant's visit can educate staff and raise the standards of handling and care with a minimum of disruption.

REFERENCES

Chapter I

1. A. Davanne and J. Girard, *Recherches Theoriques et Pratiques sur la Formation des Èpreuves Positives Photographiques* (Paris: Gauthier-Villars, 1864), pp. 3-7.

2. James M. Reilly, *The Albumen and Salted Paper Book: The History and Practice of Photographic Printing 1845-1895* (Rochester, New York: Light Impressions Corporation, 1980), p. 47.

3. James M. Reilly, "The Manufacture and Use of Albumen Paper," *The Journal of Photographic Science*, Vol. 26 (1978), pp. 156-161.

4. P. F. Mathieu, *Auto-Photographie ou Méthod de Reproduction par la Lumière des Dessins, Lithographies, Gravures, etc.* (Paris: 1847), p. 14.

5. Anonymous, "Winter Printing from Paper Negatives," *The Photographic News*, Vol. 3, No. 65 (1859), p. 145. See also R. B. Rogett, "Development Printing," *Photographic Notes*, Vol. 5, No. 4 (1860), p. 72.

6. J. S. Butler, "Solar Printing By Development," *The Photographer's Friend*, Vol. 1 (1871) Supplement, p. 21.

7. Josef M. Eder and Fritz Wentzel, *Die photographischen Kopirverfahren mit Silbersalzen (Positiv-Prozess)* (Halle: Verlag von Wilhelm Knapp, 1928), p. 110.

8. E. A. Kusel, *The Philadelphia Photographer*, Vol. 6, No. 64 (1869), pp. 111-113.

9. Edward L. Wilson, "Printing Methods and Formulae," *Photographic Mosaics*, Vol. 32 (1896), p. 58.

10. J. M. Eder and F. Wentzel, *op. cit.*, pp. 134-183.

11. F. C. Beach, "Bromide Paper for Positive Prints, and An Apparatus for Enlargements," *The Photographic News*, Vol. 30, No. 1435 (1886), p. 155.

12. Paul Hanneke, *Das Celloidinpapier* (Berlin: Verlag von Gustav Schmidt, 1897), p. 5.

13. G. F. Joubert, "The Progress of Photography and the Processes of Photo-Mechanical Printing," *The Philadelphia Photographer*, Vol. 28, No. 8 (1896), p. 357.

14. J. A. Tennant, "Development Printing Papers," *The Photo-Miniature*, Vol. 14, No. 46 (1903).

Chapter II

15. J. Reilly, N. Kennedy, D. Black, and T. Van Dam, "Image Structure and Deterioration in Albumen Prints," *Photographic Science and Engineering*, Vol. 28, No. 4 (1984), pp. 166-171.

16. C. R. Berry and D. C. Skillman, "The Color and Covering Power of Silver Particles," *The Journal of Photographic Science*, Vol. 17 (1969), pp. 145-149.

17. T. H. James and W. Vanselow, "The Influence of the Development Mechanism on the Color and Morphology of Developed Silver," *Photographic Science and Engineering*, Vol. 1, No. 3 (1958), pp. 104-118.

18. A. Haddon and F. B. Grundy, "On the Amounts of Silver and Hypo Left in Albumenised Paper at Different Stages of Washing," *British Journal of Photography*, Vol. 40 (1893), pp. 511-512.

19. Thomas Hardwich, *A Manual of Photographic Chemistry*, 3rd ed. (London: John Churchill, 1856), p. 168.

20. J. M. Reilly, D. Severson, and C. McCabe, "Image Deterioration in Albumen Prints," in Preprints of the 9th International Congress of the IIC, *Science and Technology in the Service of Conservation* (London: IIC, 1982), pp. 61-65.

21. Larry Feldman, "Discoloration of Black-and-White Photographic Prints," *Journal of Applied Photographic Engineering*, Vol. 7, No. 1 (1981), pp. 1-9.

22. E. Steven Brandt, "Mechanistic Studies of Silver Image Stability 1. Redox Chemistry of Oxygen and Hydrogen Peroxide at Clean and Adsorbate-Covered Silver Electrodes," *Photographic Science and Engineering*, Vol. 28, No. 1 (1984), pp. 1-12.

23. W. E. Lee, F. J. Drago, and A. T. Ram, "New Procedures for the Processing and Storage of KODAK Spectroscopic Plates, Type III a-J," *Journal of Applied Photographic Engineering*, Vol. 10 (1984), pp. 22-28.

24. Y. Minagawa and M. Torigoe, "Some Factors Influencing the Discoloration of Black and White Photographs in Hydrogen Peroxide Atmosphere," Paper Presented at the SPSE International Symposium on the Stability and Preservation of Photographic Images, Ottawa, 1982.

25. Klaus Hendriks, *The Preservation and Restoration of Photographic Materials in Libraries and Archives (a RAMP Study with Guidelines)* (Paris: UNESCO, 1984), p. 46.

26. Thomas Hardwich, *op. cit.*, p. 135.

27. W. E. Lee, B. Wood, and F. J. Drago, "Toner Treatments for Photographic Images to Enhance Image Stability," *Imaging Technology* (Formerly *Journal of Applied Photographic Engineering*), Vol. 10, No. 3 (1984), pp. 119-126.

28. Thomas Brill, *Light--Its Interaction with Art and Antiquities* (New York: Plenum Press, 1980), p. 223.

29. Alfred S. Taylor, "Experiments on Carbon Prints," *The Illustrated Photographer*, Vol. 1 (1868), p. 415.

30. Sergio Burgi, "Fading of Dyes Used for Tinting Unsensitized Albumen Paper," Paper Presented at the SPSE International Symposium on the Stability and Preservation of Photographic Images, Ottawa, 1982.

31. J. M. Reilly, "Role of the Maillard, or 'Protein-Sugar' Reaction in Highlight Yellowing of Albumen Prints," in Preprints of Papers Presented at the 10th Annual Meeting of the American Institute for Conservation, Milwaukee, 1982, pp. 160-168.

32. Bernard Idson and Emily Braswell, "Gelatin," *Advances in Food Research*, Vol. 7 (1957), pp. 235-338.

33. J. M. Eder and F. Wentzel, *op. cit.*, pp. 227-314.

34. Anne F. Clapp, *Curatorial Care of Works of Art on Paper*, 3rd rev. ed. (Oberlin: Intermuseum Laboratory, 1978), pp. 3-48.

35. Alice Swan, "Conservation of Photographic Print Collections," *Library Trends*, Vol. 30, No. 2 (1981), pp. 267-296.

Chapter III

36. Anne Cartier-Bresson, *Les Papiers Salés* (Paris: Direction des Affaires Culturelles de la Ville de Paris, 1984), pp. 66-79.

37. Lucia Tang, "Determination of Iron and Copper Content in 18th and 19th Century Books by Flameless Atomic Absorption Spectroscopy," *Journal of the American Institute for Conservation*, Vol. 17, No. 2 (1978), pp. 19-32.

38. Anonymous, *The Photographic News*, Vol. 17, No. 762 (1873), pp. 174-175.

39. Debbie Hess Norris, "Eakins at Avondale: Discovery, Examination and Treatment of His Platinum Prints," Preprints of Papers Presented at the 8th Annual Meeting of the American Institute for Conservation, San Francisco, 1980, pp. 53-61.

40. Nora Kennedy and James M. Reilly, Lecture Presentation During the Photographic Materials Group Session of the American Institute for Conservation, Baltimore, May 1983.

41. George T. Eaton, "Preservation of Photographic Images," *The Library Quarterly*, Vol. 40, No. 1 (1970), pp. 55-98.

Chapter V

42. Margery S. Long, "Appraisal and Collecting Policies," in *Administration of Photographic Collections* (Chicago: Society of American Archivists, 1984), pp. 55-70.

43. Joan Pedzich, "Balancing Preservation and Research: Some Principles That Help," *PhotographiConservation*, Vol. 4, No. 2 (1982), pp. 6-7.

44. Dennis V. Piechota and Greta Hansen, "The Care of Cultural Property in Transit: A Case Design for Traveling Exhibitions," *Studies in Conservation*, Vol. 7, No. 4 (1982), pp. 32-46.

45. John E. Hunter, "Museum Disaster Planning," *Museum, Archive, and Library Security*, ed. Lawrence J. Fennelly (Boston: Butterworths, 1983), pp. 235-279.

46. Stephen W. Weldon, "Fire Protection Systems and Fire Protection Techniques," *Museum, Archive, and Library Security* (Boston: Butterworths, 1983), pp. 177-234.

47. Consult the American Institute For Conservation of Historic and Artistic Works, 3545 Williamsburg Lane N. W., Washington, D.C. 20008, tel. (202) 364-1036.

48. Klaus B. Hendriks and Brian Lesser, "Disaster Preparedness and Recovery: Photographic Materials," *American Archivist*, Vol. 46, No. 1 (1983), pp. 52-68.

Chapter VI

49. Edith Weyde, "A Simple Test to Identify Gases Which Harm Silver Images," *Photographic Science and Engineering*, Vol. 16, No. 4 (1972), pp. 283-286.

50. A. F. Clapp, *op. cit.*, p. 16.

51. A. L. Romanoff, and A. J. Romanoff, *The Avian Egg* (New York: John Wiley & Sons, 1949), p. 748.

52. Garry Thomson, *The Museum Environment* (London: Butterworths, 1978), p. 85.

53. Gunter Kolf, "Modern Photographic Papers," *British Journal of Photography*, Vol. 127 (1980), pp. 316-319.

54. K. J. Macleod, *Relative Humidity: Its Importance, Measurement and Control in Museums*, The Canadian Conservation Institute, Technical Bulletin No. 1 (Ottawa, 1978).

55. Debbie Hess Norris, "The Proper Storage and Display of a Photographic Collection," *Picturescope*, Vol. 31, No. 1 (1983), pp. 4-10.

56. James M. Reilly, "Evaluation of Storage Enclosure Materials for Photographs Using the ANSI Photographic Activity Test," Final Narrative Report of Accomplishment for National Museum Act Grant #FC-309557 (March 1984).

57. American National Standard PH 1.53-1984, *American National Standard for Photography (Processing)— Processed Film, Plates and Papers— Filing Enclosures and Containers for Storage* (New York: American National Standards Institute, 1984), p. 9.

58. Margaret R. Brown, *Boxes for the Protection of Rare Books—Their Design and Construction*, (Washington, D.C.: Library of Congress, 1983).

59. Tim Padfield, David Erhardt, and Walter Hopwood, "Trouble in Store," in Preprints of the 9th International Congress of the IIC, *Science and Technology in the Service of Conservation* (London: IIC, 1982), pp. 24-27.

60. Robert Mathey, Thomas K. Faison, and Samuel Silberstein, *Air Quality Criteria for Storage of Paper-Based Archival Records*, National Bureau of Standards Publication NBSIR 83-2795 (Washington, 1983), p. 19.

Chapter VII

61. Laurance E. Keefe, Jr., and Dennis Inch, *The Life of a Photograph—Archival Processing, Matting, Framing and Storage* (Boston: Focal Press, 1984), pp. 79-141.

62. Thomas Brill, *op. cit.*, pp. 173-195.

63. Garry Thomson, *op. cit.*, p. 25.

64. Garry Thomson, *op. cit.*, p. 23.

65. Henry Wilhelm, "Monitoring the Fading and Staining of Color Photographic Prints," *Journal of the American Institute for Conservation*, Vol. 21, No. 1 (1981), pp. 49-54.

66. Siegfried Rempel, *The Care of Black-and-White Photographic Collections: Cleaning and Stabilization*, The Canadian Conservation Institute, Technical Bulletin No. 9 (Ottawa, 1980).

67. Grant Romer, "Some Notes on the Past, Present and Future of Photographic Preservation," *Image*, Vol. 27, No. 4 (1984), pp. 16-23.

BIBLIOGRAPHY

Chapter I

Abney, William de W. and Clark, Lyonel. *Platinotype—Its Preparation and Manipulation*. London: Sampson, Low and Marston, 1895.

Barger, M. Susan. *Bibliography of Photographic Processes In Use Before 1880*. Rochester, New York: The Graphic Arts Research Center, Rochester Institute of Technology, 1980.

Darrah, William Culp. *Cartes de Visite in Nineteenth Century Photography*. Gettysburg, Pennsylvania: William C. Darrah, pub., 1981.

Gernsheim, Helmut. *The History of Photography*. New York: McGraw-Hill, 1969.

Gernsheim, Helmut. *The Origins of Photography*. New York: Thames & Hudson, 1982.

Jenkins, Reese V. *Images and Enterprise*. Baltimore: The Johns Hopkins University Press, 1975.

Newhall, Beaumont. *The History of Photography*. New York: The Museum of Modern Art, 1982.

Reilly, James M. *The Albumen and Salted Paper Book: The History and Practice of Photographic Printing 1840-1895*. Rochester, New York: Light Impressions Corp., 1980.

Towler, John. *The Silver Sunbeam*, New York: J. H. Ladd, 1864 (Facsimile Edition by Morgan & Morgan, Hastings on Hudson, 1969).

Wentzel, Fritz. *Memoirs of a Photochemist*. Philadelphia: American Museum of Photography, 1960.

Wilson, Edward. *The American Carbon Manual*. New York: Scovill Manufacturing Company, 1868 (Reprinted by Arno Press, New York, 1973).

Woodbury, Walter E. *Aristotypes and How to Make Them*. New York: The Scovill and Adams Co., 1893. (Note: "Aristotypes" was a term with two meanings. To European authors such as Woodbury, it referred to gelatin printing-out paper. In America, the term usually referred to *collodion printing-out papers*.)

Chapter II

Eastman Kodak Company. *Conservation of Photographs* (Publication F-40). Rochester, New York, 1985.

Haist, Grant. *Modern Photographic Processing*. New York: John Wiley and Sons, 1979.

James, T. H., ed. *The Theory of the Photographic Process*, 4th ed. New York: MacMillan, 1972.

Plenderleith, H. J. and Werner, E. A. *The Conservation of Antiquities and Works of Art*, 2nd ed. London: Oxford University Press, 1971.

Romanoff, A. L. and Romanoff, A. J. *The Avian Egg*. New York: John Wiley and Sons, 1979.

Wall, A. H. *A Manual of Artistic Coloring as Applied to Photographs*. London: Thomas Piper, 1861 (Reprinted by Arno Press, New York, 1973).

Chapter III

Albright, Gary. "Photographs," *Conservation in the Library*, ed. Susan Swartzburg. Westport, Connecticut: Greenwood Press, 1983, pp. 79-102.

Cartier-Bresson, Anne. *Les Papiers Salés—altération et restauration des premières photographies sur papier*. Paris: Direction de Affaires Culturelles de la Ville de Paris, 1984.

Hendriks, Klaus B. *The Preservation and Restoration of Photographic Materials in Archives and Libraries: A RAMP Study with Guidelines*. Paris: UNESCO, 1984.

Swan, Alice. *The Care and Conservation of Photographic Material*. London: The Crafts Council, 1981.

Chapter IV

Coe, Brian and Haworth-Booth, Mark. *A Guide to Early Photographic Processes*. London: The Victoria and Albert Museum, 1983.

Crawford, William. *The Keepers of Light: A History and Working Guide to Early Photographic Processes*. Dobbs Ferry, New York: Morgan & Morgan, 1979.

Gill, Arthur T. *Photographic Processes, A Glossary and Chart for Their Recognition*. Museums Association (87 Charlotte St., London, W1P 2BX), Information Sheet No. 21. London: 1978.

Rempel, Siegfried. *The Care of Black-and-White Photographic Collections: Identification of Processes*. The Canadian Conservation Institute, Technical Bulletin No. 6. Ottawa: 1979.

Chapter V

Fennelly, Lawrence J., ed. *Museum, Archive, and Library Security.* Boston: Butterworths, 1983.

Kemp, Toby. "Disaster Assistance Bibliography: Selected References for Cultural/Historic Facilities." *Technology and Conservation*, Vol. 8, No. 2 (1983), pp. 25-27.

Morrow, Carolyn Clark. *The Preservation Challenge—A Guide to Conserving Library Materials.* White Plains: Knowledge Industry Publications, 1983.

Museums for a New Century. Washington, D. C.: American Association of Museums, 1984.

Ritzenthaler, Mary Lynn, Munoff, Gerald and Long, Margery. *Administration of Photographic Collections.* Chicago: Society of American Archivists, 1984.

Weinstein, Robert and Booth, Larry. *Collection, Use, and Care of Historical Photographs.* Nashville: American Association for State and Local History, 1977.

Chapter VI

Albright, Gary. "Which Envelope? Selecting Storage Enclosures for Photographs." *Picturescope*, Vol. 35 (1985), pp. 111-113.

American National Standard PH 1.48-1982, *American National Standard for Photography (Film and Slides)—Black-and-White Photographic Paper Prints—Practice for Storage.* New York: American National Standards Institute, 1984.

American National Standard PH 1.53-1984, *American National Standard for Photography (Processing)—Processed Films, Plates and Papers—Filing Enclosures and Containers for Storage.* New York: American National Standards Institute, 1984.

La Fontaine, R. H. *Recommended Environmental Monitors for Museums, Archives and Art Galleries.* The Canadian Conservation Institute, Technical Bulletin No. 3. Ottawa: 1970.

Mathey, R. G., Faison, T. K. and Silberstein, S. *Air Quality Criteria for Storage of Paper-Based Archival Records.* National Bureau of Standards Publication NBS 83-2795. Washington, D.C.: 1983.

Thomson, Garry. *The Museum Environment.* London: Butterworths, 1978.

Chapter VII

Cunha, George and Cunha, Dorothy. *Library and Archives Conservation: 1980s and Beyond*, Vols. 1 & 2. Metuchen, New Jersey: The Scarecrow Press, 1983.

Keefe, Laurance and Inch, Dennis. *The Life of a Photograph—Archival Processing, Matting, Framing and Storage.* Boston: Focal Press, 1984.

Rempel, Siegfried. *The Care of Black-and-White Photographic Collections: Cleaning and Stabilization.* The Canadian Conservation Institute, Technical Bulletin No. 9. Ottawa: 1980.

Smith, Merrily. *Matting and Hinging Works of Art on Paper.* Washington, D. C.: Library of Congress Preservation Office, 1981.